GOD'S HEART FOR THE POOR

God's Heart for the Poor

PHILIPPA STROUD
AND
CHRISTINE LEONARD

KINGSWAY PUBLICATIONS
EASTBOURNE

First published 1999

ISBN 0 85476 825 4

Published by
KINGSWAY PUBLICATIONS
Lottbridge Drove, Eastbourne, BN23 6NT, England.
E-mail: books@kingsway.co.uk

Cover design by Pinnacle Creative

Designed and produced for the publishers by
Bookprint Creative Services, P.O. Box 827, BN21 3YJ, England.
Printed in Great Britain.

Dedication

For David Stroud, who has believed in me, confronted
me, loved me, supported me, inspired me and led me
throughout the birth of the project

and

for David Devenish, who provided me with the
environment, scope and opportunity to turn what
God had put within me into reality.

Contents

IMPORTANT NOTE

While every care has been taken to ensure that the advice given in this book is both practical and complies with legal requirements, the reader is advised to check carefully with their local Citizens Advice Bureau or Social Services for any changes in the law since publication.

Preface

This is a true story and some names have been changed to protect those who have been so courageous in allowing us to write about them. My thanks to them, and especially to my staff, without whom this whole thing would not have been possible. I so appreciate your long-term faithfulness.

This is the story of how we have learnt from the many mistakes we've made and in that sense I've tried also to make it a practical 'How to' book, incorporating some of the training material which I have developed over the years. I've given various information – anything specific to Britain is in the Appendices. I've checked this information in an effort to make it as accurate as possible, but do re-check before acting upon it as situations and the law change, and neither we nor the publishers can accept any responsibility for mistakes made as a result.

PHILIPPA STROUD

1

Help! But How?

'Stop, David!' I said. 'That woman's going to fall into the road any moment.'

We were driving back, late at night, through central Bedford. The woman was staggering about from one side of the pavement to the other, obviously high on something and missing the fast-moving traffic purely by accident.

'Do you have any ideas of what we can do for her?' David wanted to know, once he'd pulled the car up safely.

'Take her back to my flat!'

He looked at me. 'Where are you going to put her?'

'There's room – one of the girls is away – and we have a responsibility to help!'

I felt torn. I knew David had been looking forward to snatching a few moments with me before parting for the night. We'd had so little chance to spend time together since deciding to marry. For the last month we'd at least been in the same country, but our heavy work schedules had left little time to catch up with one another. And now I was asking him to help me transport this frail woman back to my flat. We knew nothing about her. It occurred to me that she could knife us, or be violently ill, but I knew we needed to reach out and care for her, because we had the means to help. Both of us understood that this individual, though frail, was as valuable and unique as anyone and wanted her to experience something of God's love for her.

As we walked up to her, we could see she was clutching a slim aerosol of hairspray as though her life depended on it, and in a way it did. Sniffing it had already made her suffer dangerous consequences. How old was she, I wondered. Seventy? Though tiny enough to be a child, she looked ancient, but I judged she'd be nearer fifty-five. As we led her gently towards the car she responded without aggression, in a daze.

I shivered. Apart from anything else, I knew that if she stayed out in this piercing March wind she'd be seriously at risk. We explained we were taking her somewhere safe and warm for the night, but doubted that she understood a word we said. As we helped her into the car, the harsh orange light revealed a purple bruise all down the left side of her face. She'd been hit, and recently. I watched her carefully, wondering who were the important people in her life. Where did she sleep and eat? What moved her, hurt her, brought her joy? Or was she numb? She remained silent. We didn't even know her name.

Back at the flat, David kissed me goodnight, then departed, while my flatmate Nicki helped me tuck the woman into the spare bed. The next morning she awoke frightened, with no idea of how she had come to be there. We did our best to reassure her, but she wanted to leave. We learnt only that her name was Karina.

We may have kept her safe that night but we had come nowhere near understanding the root of her problems. I felt frustrated we'd not been able to do more. A couple of years later I saw her picture in the paper under the headline 'Bag woman murdered'. The journalist described her as a 'well-known drinker and derelict' and the photograph showed, once again, cuts and bruises on the left side of her face.

What did it take, I wondered, to connect someone like Karina with the salvation she so desperately needed? Could ordinary Christians in an ordinary church in an ordinary English town like Bedford really work effectively with people like her? There seemed so big a gap, and yet everything in the Bible suggested that God urges his people to be a voice for the voiceless, not only to love and care for them but to walk with them through their pain and conflicts until they became radical disciples of Jesus. Could it work, here and now? I knew we couldn't expect results overnight, but what kind of long-term commitment would it take? What were the costs? Those are the questions I asked then, and they are the questions I want to look at in this book.

I first met Mary one Saturday morning in 1989, shortly after Karina had stayed with us. Hands stuffed in the pockets of an over-tight denim jacket, Mary leant against the wall by Sainsbury's, facing away from all the noise we were making. Unlike most passers-by, she appeared to have no curiosity about our street painting, the drama group or David's speaking – yet she kept hanging around Pigeon Square, where she couldn't avoid hearing us.

Eventually David started talking to her. After a few moments he called me over.

'Mary, this is my fiancée, Philippa. I met her in Hong Kong.'

She stared at me.

David continued, 'Mary used to come to my church youth group about – what? – ten years ago?'

She managed a nod but her eyes were dull.

David continued, 'So, what's been happening with you over the years, Mary?'

She started shaking, an overweight woman in her mid-twenties, with unkempt hair and dirty trainers. Then she muttered that she'd been married for some time. 'Not that it's made me happy!'

'Are things pretty bad then?' David asked.

'Jim's up on a court charge. Caught for possessing arms and ammunition,' she admitted.

I thought of something practical that I might be able to do to reach someone so needy yet so aloof.

'How are you feeling about going to court?' I asked.

'Terrified.'

She didn't have to say the word.

'Do you have any family who'll go with you?'

'That lot? Couldn't give a …!'

'Would it help if I came with you?' I was trying to find some way to show her that I cared.

'I have to go to Northampton.'

I knew there was no Crown Court in Bedford. 'That doesn't matter. I'll drive you there and sit with you, if you think that would help.'

'Would you?' Maybe it was her surprise that made her look at me properly for the first time. 'That'd be cool.'

When we arrived at the court it happened that she wasn't on her own at all. A large group of mates had come along for support and she introduced me to them as 'a friend from Hong Kong'. Then of course I had to explain what a twenty-two-year-old English girl had been doing out there.

'I was helping some addicts go through drug withdrawal,' I explained.

'I've got a mate who's blatantly taking too much dope,' said one man, whose dilated pupils indicated that perhaps his friend wasn't the only one with the problem. 'D'you think you could help him, then?'

We spent most of that day – Mary, her friends and I – waiting around at the court. I enjoyed being with them, listening to their stories and hearing about their worlds. Most of them seemed very accepting of my intrusion.

One guy showed some antagonism. 'Look at you, in your pearls. What d'you know about our life? You can't speak all posh like you speak and understand us!'

'You try her,' said Mary.

'Bet you found it tough, though, working with addicts!' another woman cut in.

'No, I loved it!'

'So, did they stick it out?'

'Well yes, many of them did!' It seemed natural to tell them about the power of Jesus and the Holy Spirit to bring people off drugs painlessly and then turn their lives around for the better.

'Pah, religion!' said one of the guys. 'That's not for me.'

'I used to feel like that!' I said, and went on talking about Jackie Pullinger and the work we'd been doing. I told them how Chinese men from Triad gangs changed after they'd met Jesus – and they kept asking me questions. When they asked if it could work the same way in England, I said yes, because God is the same everywhere and he cares about everyone, not just the 'nice' people who go to church.

Some of them didn't want to know, and Mary tried to hush their more colourful forms of expression.

'A few rude words won't worry her!' laughed one of them.

Most were genuinely interested in Jesus and asked if I could help. Not them, they said, they were fine. It was their friends who had problems.

It was as though in offering to spend a day in court with Mary I had caught hold of a tiny thread – a thread that had led to a vast, tangled mess made up of individual lives. It seemed that some of these people knew they needed the Jesus who said he had come to bring good news to the oppressed, to bind up the broken-hearted, to proclaim liberty to the captives and release to the prisoners. They might not have acknowledged it at the time but they needed the God who cared passionately for the poor and marginalised, who cared for those who were 'stuck', for those who had no real voice or means of changing things for themselves. They needed a God who would rescue people from the mess in which they found themselves, whether or not it was of their own making.

I knew that God could turn people like Mary's friends into those capable of working with him to rescue others. I had seen it happen. If it could work in Hong Kong, then it could work in Bedford. This is what I wanted and, because I knew it could happen, I prayed that we would see it here.

Over the next months I saw a good deal of that group, and their friends – and I spent an enormous amount of time with Mary. In fact the court didn't send Jim to prison then – that happened for a different offence later. But I found out that Mary's problems didn't centre only around the court case, or the fact that she and Jim were for ever in debt and in trouble with their landlord. When I realised that Jim kept beating her up and that she needed a safe place to live, I invited her to stay for a while in the flat I was sharing with Nicki and Meryl – two girls from our church – having talked it over with them first, of course.

For me the flat was merely somewhere to live for a short while before my wedding, but the others had worked hard and imaginatively, making pretty curtains and creating a comfortable home. Nicki, a qualified social worker, cared for mentally disturbed adults, while Meryl was doing a year's full-time service on our church's Evangelism Team. My fiancé, David, led the team, and I knew how hard he worked them! I was working for the church too, with the Team's contacts on the estates who needed extra pastoral care. I was also trying to help Mary's friends and reaching out to their friends and others I'd met on the streets.

Though the flat wasn't luxurious, after our demanding days the others could relax there in relative peace and quiet – until Mary arrived. Very grateful at first, soon she began making constant demands on our attention, creating an icy atmosphere if we refused to drop everything that very moment. 'You never have cared about me. You just want to get on with your own lives!' she would accuse us. While she rarely acknowledged that we did anything right, things which went wrong in her life were all our fault.

She worked making sausages in a meat factory but, after she stormed out of there once too often, she found herself unemployed. When she started hanging round the flat all day, its atmosphere changed. She sulked, for days sometimes, or she would storm off back to Jim, 'the only person who ever loved me', only to get beaten all over again and reappear in a worse state than ever. Then she became even more ferocious in her demands for our affirmation.

We discovered further layers of the tangle when she admitted to previous lesbian relationships and to being on the receiving end of abuse from her family. I could see why she was in a mess! But, although we tried to help her through all these things, we saw little improvement. She did try to respond but, having received unhelpful counselling for her deep-seated problems in the past, she wouldn't contemplate that route again. By huge efforts of the will she would manage to curb her problems with drink and money for a while – then she'd lose her grip and sink further than ever.

All three of us found the situation draining. We had to steel ourselves to go back to the flat at the end of the day and face whatever might be thrown at us. Nicki coped brilliantly, considering that her work made tremendous demands on her emotions. She needed her own time and space to recharge her batteries, yet Mary often turned to her for help, since they'd known each other from early days in the youth club. Soon the strain began to tell, and I began to wonder how you did this thing twenty-four hours a day for months on end. Meryl too was struggling – I think anyone would have struggled in similar circumstances – and eventually she became ill. I wondered how one person could have this effect on three sane, mature graduates.

I felt responsible for bringing Mary into the flat in the

first place, but still the questions which plagued me wouldn't go away. 'How on earth do we help someone like her?' I kept asking myself. 'Even with God on our side, can one person, or even three, untangle the mess of problems which have built up over so many years? We've prayed, we've shared our faith with her, we've tried our best to show her love. We've given and given of ourselves – and when she's thrown it all back in our faces, we've given again. What more can we sacrifice? What else does she need, Lord?'

As I looked through the Bible, I could see promise after promise which should have helped Mary but, when I looked at her life, the gap between the two seemed unbridgeable. I had no idea how to bring her into her rightful inheritance, into all that I believed that Jesus had bought for her with his life's blood. In fact it seemed that my efforts had succeeded only in putting myself and my flatmates under levels of strain which were damaging us. We kept trying to help people – Mary and Karina were not the only ones. Yet we had so little to show for it, and we'd been burnt ourselves.

My frustration grew because I knew from my experiences in Hong Kong that lives every bit as damaged as Mary's could be transformed when Jesus' love and power were mediated through his people, and yet it wasn't happening here. At the end of myself, I turned to him again.

'My heart cries out for those who do not know you,' I prayed, 'for those who do not know the joy of receiving your love, for those who walk in darkness. You know I long to see your kingdom extended in David's work and in my work. May your will be done, Father. We commit all of ourselves in obedience. May we see your power poured out. May we see your potential demonstrated in human lives. May we see scripture fulfilled in our day!

'I feel so small for the task to which you have called me. I look at it and my heart feels fearful for I can see so clearly how powerless I am to do it. And yet your promise to me is that I shall not be drowned, that I need not fear for I am your child, I belong to you. You are my God. Your presence alone brings power, brings peace, brings love.'

God did answer that prayer in the end. Along the route though, as with Mary and Karina, we were to make many mistakes, most of them avoidable. By God's grace we learnt from them, eventually, but it's so much easier to lay the foundations *before* constructing the building! I'm writing this book because I'm convinced that God is calling Christians to get involved with some kind of ministry with the poor, preferably through their local church. I'm hoping it will show how to build good foundations for this kind of work, and show something of how you could do it.

We've not ended up with anything spectacular in Bedford, but we did build a church where a rich businessman can sit alongside someone living rough on the streets, a church where Christians are learning together how to care for the broken – and growing themselves in the process. Many have received a measure of healing and a small percentage have come right through to become radical disciples of Jesus. Some have become church leaders or are reaching out to bring God's healing to other lives. But this isn't about numbers, it's about obedience to a God who says, 'In as much as you did it to the least of these my brothers you did [or did not do] it to me' (Matthew 25:40).

2

A Heart for the Poor

Back in 1989, hoping for some answers, I let my mind spin back to my time in Hong Kong – but things hadn't always been easy there either. After a great send-off from friends and family in England, reality hit me when a whole tribe of Chinese people surged into the airport departure lounge. I could not understand a single word of their noisy conversation. I knew that I would have to learn Chinese, of course, but this was the first time I realised what it might mean to live in an alien environment. I stared at them. Do I *like* Chinese people, I found myself wondering? I couldn't turn back now and yet … why on earth was I doing this?

Sure, a number of Christians I knew had suggested I might work with Jackie Pullinger – so many that I had to concede God must be speaking. These people weren't colluding – most didn't even know each other. But the only thing I had heard God say to me personally was, 'Go sell all you have and give it to the poor.' For a whole year nearly every time I opened the Bible those words leapt out and hit me hard between the eyes. At the time I was studying at a French university. Like all students, I had hardly any money and nothing to sell. Frustration built within me. What did God mean? I'd have done anything, gone anywhere, to find out!

I'd been a Christian for a couple of years. I knew that God loved me, cared for me and, above all, listened to me, but I wondered how I could ever love him in return. 'How can a finite being love an infinite God?' I asked him, over and over again until I read, 'If you love me, you will obey what I command' (John 14:15).

'That's how people love me, Philippa, through obedience,' he said. That was when I realised that obeying him had to be the guiding principle of my life. I had been bought with a price. My life was no longer my own but was to be lived in obedience to him. Now he was asking me to do something I couldn't do – or could I? Though as a student I lacked possessions, I would soon have considerable earning potential. I used to work in the City in the holidays. I'd assumed I'd follow my father into a career in the financial world and enjoy a comfortable lifestyle, like all of my friends. But although I knew I'd do well at it, banking didn't fill me with passion.

'Why all this about the poor, God?' I asked. 'You let other Christians enjoy the lifestyles they want – nice houses in the country, a great time socially and Sunday worship. OK, maybe I would want more, but how come they're satisfied and I'm not? What's with all this poor business?'

And here I was, with no money again, on the way to Hong Kong, to work among drug addicts and criminals. It wasn't that I wanted to, particularly. I was simply doing my best to obey God. But even before the plane skimmed low over the Walled City on its approach to

Hong Kong airport, I started to feel excited. Emerging from the air-conditioned Kaitak terminal I hit a wall of heat and humidity. Never mind jet lag, the skyscraper city electrified me as it sparked colour, noise, energy and movement twenty-four hours a day. The laid-back guy who drove me to Hang Fook Camp must have found me unbearable as I fired question after question about what to him were everyday details.

I was itching to start work straight away, to learn and to become part of this place, to fill my senses, my mind and my life with it. I felt particularly drawn to the Walled City, called in Chinese 'Hak Nam' – 'Darkness'. But at Hang Fook Camp, the base of Jackie's work, they told me to take twenty-four hours off to recover from the flight. Then I learnt that Jackie Pullinger, this woman the Lord seemed so keen for me to meet, had gone on an extended ministry trip to South Africa.

'What would you like me to do?' I asked eagerly after my enforced rest. Yelling, 'Let me at it!' would have expressed my feelings better.

'We really need someone to answer telephone calls in the office,' they told me. Oh! My mind flipped back to church meetings in England where people had prayed for me. We'd all assumed I'd be working with dangerous drug addicts, with murderers and gang leaders deep in the foul darkness of the Walled City, where few Westerners venture!

I swallowed hard. Maybe God was teaching me about being faithful in small things. OK, then, I'd be the most helpful, friendly and co-operative telephone answerer they'd ever had! I'd make everyone the most superlative coffee and, if photocopying or anything needed doing around the office, I'd do it efficiently and with a smile. I'd even do the Bulletin (not my kind of thing at all!). But in the meanwhile, maybe I could go to the Walled City services of a Sunday?

'Sorry, Philippa,' they told me, 'but we can't flood that with Westerners. We let in just three at a time, on a strict rotation. Your turn will come, but not yet.'

Determined not to let apparent setbacks put me off, I chose to find inspiration in the office's writing paper. It featured a bamboo cross and tiny words from Isaiah printed both in English and Chinese. Each time I used a sheet of that paper the words confronted me and clarified my calling. Gradually everything started to make sense.

'"Is not this the kind of fasting I have chosen: to loose the chains of injustice and untie the cords of the yoke, to set the oppressed free and break every yoke? Is it not to share your food with the hungry and to provide the poor wanderer with shelter – when you see the naked, to clothe him, and not to turn away from your own flesh and blood? Then your light will break forth like the dawn, and your healing will quickly appear; then your righteousness will go before you, and the glory of the Lord will be your rear guard. Then you will call, and the Lord will answer; you will cry for help, and he will say: Here am I"' (Isaiah 58:6–9).

So this was it then, God had chosen this way. It was his choice for those who followed him that we should set the oppressed free and share our food with the hungry. I'd always thought that care for the poor and speaking out against injustice were some kind of optional extra for left-wing Christians – fine if that's your thing, but not for everyone. But if this was the way that God had *chosen*, then there was no other way.

' "If you do away with the yoke of oppression, with the pointing finger and malicious talk, and if you spend yourselves on behalf of the hungry and satisfy the needs of the oppressed, then your light will rise in the darkness, and your night will become like the noonday. The Lord will guide you always; he will satisfy your needs in a sun-scorched land and will strengthen your frame. You will be like a well-watered garden, like a spring whose waters never fail. Your people will rebuild the ancient ruins and will raise up the age-old foundations; you will be called Repairer of Broken Walls, Restorer of Streets with Dwellings...." The mouth of the Lord has spoken' (Isaiah 58:9–12, 14).

So it wasn't something to be done in convenient parcels of time like Saturday afternoons. Nor would God be content with a gap year between university and starting a career. No, he was asking us to spend our very selves on behalf of the hungry, to share our food and clothes and whole lives with them. He was calling us – not to poverty, for we find riches in him – but to embrace poverty.

I'd never thought that care for the poor would take over my whole life, though looking back I can see certain pointers in incidents from my past. Some friends bought me a subscription to *National Geographic* magazine for my eighth birthday and I remember lying across a massive Queen Anne armchair in our house in France, transfixed for a good couple of hours by photographs of famine victims from Bangladesh. I wondered about the lives of these emaciated children of my own age, whose bodies didn't even have folds where mine did. I wanted so much to go and help them, but of course that wasn't practical for an eight-year-old.

I think I've always reacted like that. Action-orientated, I always want to find a solution to suffering and find it hard when external constraints stop me.

A greater influence were my parents, who believed in action too. My mother worked as a sister in a cancer hospice. My father's international banking took him abroad a good deal and meant we lacked for nothing. When at home, he served as a Samaritan, choosing to invest his spare time with hurting people. As I grew up that seemed normal, and only later did I realise how unusual he was.

When Idi Amin expelled the Asians from Uganda, my mother volunteered to help in the refugee camp which was set up near where we lived in Surrey. When I was about five or six I spent some of my holidays with her there in the big old army barracks. I thought it was great getting to know the Asian kids. They would take me off to meet their families who huddled around one bed with all their pots and pans and other possessions. I loved the freedom of being able to roam like that. I found it exciting, especially sampling food so different from anything I'd eaten before. And while I saw real illness, real suffering, I also saw people doing plenty to help.

The Government dealt with a later influx of Vietnamese refugees by asking English people to 'adopt' a family. I remember, at the age of about twelve, helping to scrub out a house, then to collect furniture and move it in. 'Our' Vietnamese family arrived, huddled in thick jackets because they felt so cold in the British summertime. They insisted on using only one downstairs room of the house. My mother gave them language lessons and arranged the young children's schooling, while the father came to work in our garden, though we had never employed a gardener before. I guess all this left me with a sense that if anyone, even a stranger, needed help, it was normal to throw yourself into action.

And now, through obeying God's commands, I found myself in Hong Kong, living in a tin hut in the old Hang Fook refugee camp which had been given to Jackie. Others had come from all over the world. I shared a tiny bedroom there with various of them, yet somehow I felt so at home and more free to be myself than I had ever been.

My role in the office supported others who worked directly with the poor and made a real difference to their lives. I had nothing, but learnt valuable lessons about God's generous provision. For example, one day I found to my embarrassment that all my underpants had gone missing.

'Well, God, what happens now?' I prayed. 'You know I have no money!'

I walked into the camp and looked in the cupboard where they stored donations of second-hand clothing, dubious about what kind of underpants I would find there, if any! I discovered a box full of hundreds of brand new pairs, in exactly the style I would have chosen in the shops. The only slight snag was that they were factory off-cuts, all of which featured the Playboy rabbit. I used to wonder what people would think should they discover me wearing them in hospital after a road accident!

Nothing could stop me going into the Walled City during my time off. The first time I took the Underground to Lock Fu with a small group from Hang Fook, my excitement kept me unusually quiet. As we walked down the hill we saw our destination looming up like a huge wall twelve storeys high, and divided into little rectangles, each with its laundry hanging on railings to dry. I couldn't see a way inside, but my companions assured me there were several which didn't lead to dead ends but twisted through alleyways two feet wide, down flights of steps, further and further inside the labyrinth.

Sure enough they led me to one and I could see the rectangles continuing inside the structure, teetering upwards like Lego blocks. Some were little shops with lights, others tiny factories which made buttons, or charms to go in crackers. Most of the time it was too dark to see the uneven floor but it felt slimy from the open drains which ran along each side of the narrow passageway. Undaunted by our presence, rats congregated around the piles of rubbish.

Suddenly we emerged into an open area, complete with grimy tiles on the floor and a staircase leading upwards to nowhere. My companions explained that the Walled City had been built around this, a former palace. It had been left out of the treaty between China and Britain so that no one ruled there – except the Triad gangs.

I visited the Walled City often after that and soon made friends with the Chinese outreach team working there. I say 'working', but this group of six Brothers who had come off drugs and met Jesus through Jackie's work were still growing accustomed to daily structure and work routine.

After three months I was asked to help take a young woman off heroin. I set off to meet her, partnered by a seventy-year-old ex-prostitute and heroin addict who spoke no English. I was a foot taller than her four foot six inches. We must have looked a funny sight on the ferry to Macau – the Portuguese-run peninsular of mainland China.

We spent ten days with Ah Wah there as she went through withdrawal. With little Chinese and no experience of taking someone off drugs, I skimmed through my unread copy of Jackie's book, *Chasing the Dragon*, asking, 'How do you do this?'

We gave Ah Wah numerous baths. When her body ached we massaged her muscles and we prayed with her. Amazingly she experienced little pain. But by the end of that ten days she became violent and aggressive. After threatening me with a knife, she left. This was my first experience of drug withdrawal. It felt like failure.

I had to learn that God goes on caring for an individual and that he wants us to do the same. Even when no one sees us and even when everything goes wrong, that person's value remains unaltered.

Shortly after this, Jackie returned to Hong Kong and walked straight up to me in the Hang Fook office. 'So you want to live in the Walled City, do you then?' she asked.

I nearly fell off my chair but managed to say, 'Yes, yes I do!'

'OK, then, in a month's time you can come and live with me!'

Two days later Jackie slipped over in the Walled City, breaking her arm, and asked me to move in to help her straight away.

And so I found myself, at the age of twenty-two, living

with a woman of forty, sharing a tiny room on the eighth floor of a twelve-storey apartment block. The Brothers lived in the equivalent rooms on each of the two floors above.

Jackie had already spent a quarter of a century working in the rat-infested Walled City, the city which never slept. At night I could hear spitting, coughing, crying and arguing as well as noise from the tiny factories which worked twenty-four hours a day. However, the little restaurants which paid protection money to the Triads – the restaurants with their tin tables and wonderful food – closed at night. So if Jackie said she was hungry at one in the morning I'd have to cross town and go over to the edge of Kowloon to buy food. I wasn't afraid in the Walled City, but on these trips, alone at night in a strange country, I used to wonder who would notice if I went missing – and I would be praying in tongues all the way!

I was supposed to be looking after Jackie but the privilege of living so closely to her proved a challenging one. Yet her faith and her passion for the poor were contagious. She had a unique way of looking at things and believed that the result of ministering to the poor should be to help them become fully functional for God.

Jesus stated his manifesto at the beginning of his ministry on earth by quoting from Isaiah 61. Jackie believed that, as Jesus' servants, his people should continue his work. She and those working with her believed the Spirit was with them as they preached good news to the poor, bound up the broken-hearted, proclaimed freedom for the captives and released prisoners from darkness. Former homeless addicts, transformed by God into 'oaks of righteousness' for the display of his glory, would, in their turn, 'rebuild the ancient ruins ... restore the places long devastated ... renew the ruined cities that have been devastated for many generations' (Isaiah 61:4). Using the drug rehabilitation work as a discipleship training school, Jackie would stake her life that the most dissolute individual could become a powerful missionary force for God.

From Jackie I learnt that it did work – that the power of God could not only take people off drugs painlessly but mend and transform their broken lives until they became pastors and evangelists, bringing his love to others. Her vision for the Walled City, where darkness and oppression and poverty ruled, was that God would transform it into a fragrant garden, where young and old could play together. (In fact, the Walled City was pulled down after I left. Improbable as it sounds, on that site next to the airport, the authorities planted a garden in its place.) None of this happened easily or without setbacks, but then nor did Jesus' work. I saw that it cost everything – not so much in money, but in lives given in total obedience to him.

I learnt so much by watching and taking part. Helpers were expected to pray in tongues in four-hour shifts as people came off drugs. Five years old as a Christian, I knew about the gospel, about redemption and forgiveness – and I loved the Bible. But I began to become aware of the dynamics of the Holy Spirit as I saw amazing things happen in Hong Kong. Even had I wanted to, I couldn't have stayed observing on the sideline.

At church Jackie's helpers had to sit in the front row, interceding, but whenever she preached about having a heart for the poor I would find myself trying to restrain my sobbing. Acutely embarrassed because I'd never seen this kind of thing happen to anyone else, I couldn't stop the Spirit of God coming upon me, breaking my heart. I remember being pole-axed when Jackie spoke on laying down our lives and dying to self.

The evangelical Christians I knew back in England loved Scripture but this Holy Spirit seemed to specialise in turning lives upside down and disrupting the most ordered plans. If I went this route, I realised, it meant all or nothing. Though I'd adored living in London, I knew that I wouldn't be able to return to the business environment there as though nothing had happened. If I let go of the way I'd been brought up and followed the Holy Spirit, I could end up anywhere! I feared I'd probably end my days in some Communist prison camp, like the Russians whose biographies had attracted me to Christianity in the first place.

I spent my days working, not with Jackie, but hitting grim reality with the outreach team, trying to get them out of bed in the morning to pray or evangelise. Leading from behind never did work well. As the new girl I had no authority, but had been put there to learn from them.

I'd walk the long way round to go in or out of the Walled City, so that I could chat to the ladies in the prostitutes' alley. I got to know the old ones, but the young remained incarcerated within their curtained partitions behind barred windows. I couldn't achieve much on my own.

I remember visiting one old lady whose flesh was rotting from sitting in her own urine. We cleaned and bathed her while her granddaughter watched us from the corner of the single room and played with a flea-infested kitten. Her addict son burst in just as we were trying to give the old lady something to eat and drink. Using threats, he demanded money from her.

I wanted to do something about all the suffering, so, working with the Brothers, I ended up feeling not a little frustrated. Still, nothing stopped my love of being in the Walled City. I loved it when rats ran across my feet in the dank darkness of sewer-like alleyways. I'd never felt this elation working in a bank. In the Walled City I sensed that I had come home, that for the first time in my life I could be what I was created to be. After all, wasn't this where Jesus would have chosen to spend his time, with the dirtiest of the dirty? My love of the place must have come from him for, when I returned to the Walled City later, having been in Macau for eight months, I noticed the smell for the first time and it made me nauseous.

My everyday life, though infinitely harder than it had ever been, was more caught up in God. Where Scripture had meant a great deal to my mind, at any rate, now my life depended on it. When I wanted to help someone, I searched the Bible to find out how. I needed its eternal truths – like the promise that one day I'd see Jesus face to face in heaven – to get me through each day.

After eight months Jackie said, 'You look really tired, Philippa. You need a holiday.' When I stopped to think about it, I'd given my all every day and did feel exhausted. She suggested I might like to go to a drug withdrawal house connected to her work. It was to prove quite a 'holiday'! Three years earlier Ah Ping, who had come off drugs through Jackie's work, had set this up in the nearby Portuguese-governed colony of Macau, a peninsular of mainland China. He worked among the local drug addicts, bringing them in, while a Western girl ran the house. Within twenty-four hours of my arrival, this girl decided it was time to return home to New Zealand and so I found myself in charge. My 'holiday' lasted for ten months, split into thirty-day periods of continuous twenty-four-hour duty. I had no bed, and unrolled a mattress each night on the office floor. After the thirty days I would take a four-day break in Hong Kong.

I knew I had to set an unwavering example of godly lifestyle, yet my own strength had reached breaking point right at the beginning. I had to depend on God. There was no other way through – and that pushed me into a new intimacy with Jesus. I found him faithful.

On the one hand out of my depth and lacking in every material comfort, I nevertheless proved for myself the truth of Paul's words, 'Known, yet regarded as unknown; dying, and yet we live on; beaten, and yet not killed; sorrowful, yet always rejoicing; poor, yet making many rich; having nothing, and yet possessing everything' (2 Corinthians 6:9–10).

These paradoxes brought me freedom. By losing my life I had gained it. By becoming selfless I could be more utterly myself than ever before. I thought back a few months to a bizarre incident at Waterloo Station. I'd been standing there, minding my own business, when a woman appeared from nowhere and started hitting me with her handbag. 'F***ing rich kid!' she had shouted. Yet English tourists here had been known to mistake a group of us for beggars as we walked through the streets with the Brothers. Some had even offered us money!

Leading the house in Macau proved a baptism by total immersion since I had no privacy whatsoever and had to share my whole life with these people. I was English, privileged, female, young and innocent. They were Chinese, streetwise, male, addicts and mainly older than me. At first I felt isolated, until I understood that God had placed alongside me these Christians whom he loved so much. He had given them to me as my family in Christ. *V5 to Somalians. or bread*

Ah Ping proved a phenomenal strength, as did the two other Chinese leaders, one with real pastoral skills, the other an excellent worship leader. With the work in Macau relatively new and Chinese-led, it had a different feel, perhaps more like that of Jackie's houses in the early days.

All kinds of wonderful things happened. Ah Man, a senior Triad, came off drugs and proved to be a real leader – using skills he'd learnt in the Triads! He had a good heart and loved action and activity, whether in the kitchen – where he wielded an amazing wok – redecorating the house or helping a man with an amputated leg to walk again. He could read too and often spent time talking about Scripture with the others – he would become a pastor–teacher, I felt sure. It amazed me, the effect that worship, prayer and reading the Bible had on the lives of formerly hard men whose lives had been so dark.

The house in Macau provided a brilliant opportunity for me, at the age of twenty-three, to learn about leadership, motivation and caring for people – what works and what doesn't. As leader, I started to trust my gut reactions. As I prayed that God would bring to light any immorality or wrongdoing in the house, I found that the Holy Spirit would direct me to situations that needed addressing – to a potential fight or to a man smoking in the kitchen, or to someone smuggling in drugs. This spiritual intuition has stayed with me.

By the time I finished in Macau I was exhausted, but I'd learnt about how to establish an embryonic work and about how to care for and disciple new Christians from difficult backgrounds. Through hardship and isolation, God expanded my capacity to take on responsibility. As he increased my love for the poor, he taught me the value of faithfulness in small tasks and with each individual.

It worked there, but would it work in Britain?

3

Who Are the Poor?

So why did I leave Macau for Bedford, of all places? The reason was a person of my own age, by the name of David Stroud. He had arrived to work with Jackie in Hong Kong the very same day as I had, but on a different flight. We had breakfast together that first morning but took little notice of each other.

Four months later, in December, I was surprised when he included me with a group he had invited out for his birthday meal. I'd said I'd go but then, at the very time of the meal, someone had promised to talk to me about the gifts of the Holy Spirit – a whole area I knew very little about and into which I'd been catapulted headlong. The questions in my brain needed answering.

I stood David up. I must have felt guilty, because I asked him out for a meal the next month. To my surprise we got along fine. Sharing a sense of humour and both fresh out of university, we had a lot in common. Unlike others in Hong Kong, David understood my soul-searching and the points of doctrine which bothered me – his degree in theology helped. We even agreed on some contentious issues concerning ministry and discipleship.

We would walk around Hong Kong on a Saturday evening and, seeing the poverty on the streets, I'd talk to him about how I wanted to do something for these people.

'Maybe we could have a house for them one day!' I enthused, without thinking through the logistics of why he and I should ever work together in this way. He confessed his longing to plant churches where the poor were welcome, and his frustration at getting nowhere in his attempts to reach them, back in Bedford.

He told me that when he had reached the age of seventeen, Dave Devenish had taken him under his wing, recognising in him a future church-planter. Dave led Woodside Church in Bedford, which was affiliated to one of the new church movements – New Frontiers International. They had started evangelising one of the housing estates and a number of people made commitments to follow Jesus. However, many of them had serious problems with drink or drugs. The team felt they were getting nowhere. Despite the wisdom and counselling experience in the church, lives didn't change and demonic influences didn't shift. Dave Devenish discussed with David Stroud where in the world they could find people with real problems who were changing into radical disciples of Jesus. Then they thought of Jackie's work in Hong Kong.

David took a year off after university and … here he was. It took a while before we both realised that our relationship had deepened beyond the companionship of two English Christians thrown together in a strange culture. It wasn't until the May that we started going out – eleven days before David left for three months' work and training in the USA. Because he felt called to plant churches too, he was going to a Vineyard church in Chicago for the remainder of his year out.

Somehow God supplied enough money to maintain our relationship over the international phone lines until we were able to spend a couple of weeks' leave together in England, during which we got engaged. I'd determined that I wouldn't leave Hong Kong until God called me somewhere else – I certainly wouldn't leave simply to marry! I'd expected to work in India, Malaysia or the Philippines – Jackie was developing new centres all over the place. But, in that two-week holiday, David introduced me to Dave Devenish in Bedford, who told me that Woodside Church would be pleased to give me work, adding 'I can't promise any pay, though!'

By the time I returned to England, I couldn't wait. Disappointed to miss Valentine's Day, I landed on 18th February, 1989, less than six months before our marriage in the August. Up to then David and I had spent only seven-and-a-half weeks together as a couple.

His dream was to work in bedsit land in the centre of Bedford but Dave Devenish asked him to lead an NFI Frontier Team which was to be based at Woodside in the north of Bedford. Ten young people had given up a year to do full-time training in theology, ministry gifting and character development. NFI believes in practical, hands-on training, giving plenty of opportunity to work out the theoretical side through service – in this case evangelism in one of the estates in Bedford.

When David asked God about whether he should lead the team, he felt him say, 'If you do this, I will take you, in time, to the people I've called you to.'

Woodside Church employed David as a full-time evangelist to lead the team. Remembering the promised job, I asked Dave Devenish what he wanted me to do.

'Well, we've been waiting to see what you wanted to do, Philippa,' he said. 'What do you like doing?'

That was not difficult! 'I like taking people who are broken, people who have nothing, and working with them until they become contributing members of the local church,' I replied.

'Fine! Go away and do it then!'

I had been in Bedford four days!

I took a look around. It seemed an ordinary enough county town of around 100,000 people, though I learnt it was the second oldest borough in England – and the most cosmopolitan, with over sixty ethnic groups including large numbers of Italians and Asians. I found that it had a number of colleges and a university, with both middle-class areas and council estates. Compared with Hong Kong, though, I saw few huge extremes of wealth or poverty.

In the town centre a huge statue of John Bunyan, his feet in chains, reminded me of the spiritual heritage of the place – he'd written *Pilgrim's Progress* in the old town jail. Many churches in the town flourished but, when I arrived, I found the street community unnerved by a spate of murders, which later included Karina's.

I wondered what exactly I was supposed to do. I was twenty-four years old and had been back in England just four days. Still experiencing reverse culture shock after Hong Kong, I found myself on the staff of a 300-strong church where I knew hardly a soul, charged with doing a job which lacked any guidelines.

In the end, of course, Dave Devenish and I did discuss in more detail how I might go about my work. My fiancé's Frontier Team had made many contacts on the estate, some of whom had become Christians, and now they found themselves spending more time in pastoring difficult situations than they did on evangelism.

I said, 'Give me your six most broken contacts and I'll look after them, so you can get on with what you're called to do.'

I started with six but they soon introduced me to friends and relations. Before I knew it I was looking after twelve, then eighteen, then twenty-four. A yellow Mini Metro served as my 'office' but I spent most of my days in various homes on the estate. In addition I was caring for Mary and many of her friends and for Sarah, a single mother from Woodside Church who was addicted to every tablet going.

I took Sarah off drugs in the flat which I shared with Nicki and Meryl. Complicated by the number of chemical substances involved, her withdrawal period lasted for ten days, during which I kept in close communication with her doctor. Nicki, Meryl and I took it in turns to sleep in the corridor outside her bedroom or to sit with her all night and pray. I was convinced that the same God who worked miracles with addicts in Hong Kong would work in Bedford, but it felt as if the enemy was challenging that assumption. For no apparent reason, when I was praying for Sarah, suddenly an iron fell five feet from a shelf, narrowly missing my head.

Then we appeared to win the battle. Sarah did experience the miracle of painless withdrawal through prayer. Sadly, though, she took more pills straight after leaving us and, in the end, her life failed to change very much.

In the same six-month period, life was hectic. I counselled two people who had suffered serious abuse. We sought to express the love of Jesus in every situation – on the council estate and towards people like Karina. Of course, interspersed with all this came frantic preparations for our wedding!

In the end living like this took a toll on my body and I became ill. So did David. For the nine weeks before our wedding, one or the other of us was sick. What had we to show for all our hard work? Burn-out! Clearly things weren't working so I asked Dave Devenish what I should do.

'Put a team together to help you,' he advised. David's Frontier Team was reaching the end of its time, so he suggested that I might recruit two or three of them to work for a second year with me.

Karen, Liz and Jenny agreed to do this, while supporting themselves with part-time jobs. Great, I thought, they can pastor some of my contacts. They can help with the single mothers' group I've started on Tuesday mornings and with the street guys' group on Wednesdays. Unfortunately no one thought to define what 'part-time jobs' meant, and all three found themselves working different hours. How do you run a team when its members are never available to meet or pray or train or do anything together?

Others in the church began to show interest in what we were doing and offered assistance, say for one morning a week. I hadn't learnt then that volunteer labour is not that helpful unless you can harness it properly. Volunteers looking for a slice of the action ended up disappointed when nothing happened on the two mornings when they chose to turn up. Unfortunately they weren't prepared to become key workers, on call at any time, nor to stick around doing mundane tasks such as cleaning or laundry.

This whole thing wasn't working. I began to question whether I was being presumptuous, arriving from Hong Kong wanting to help the poor in Bedford. What was I getting myself into? I asked frequently. Where would it all lead? A job in the City would have been a lot more practical!

Then I read Psalm 82: 'How long will you defend the unjust and show partiality to the wicked? Defend the cause of the weak and fatherless; maintain the rights of the poor and oppressed. Rescue the weak and needy; deliver them from the hand of the wicked. They know nothing, they understand nothing. They walk about in darkness; all the foundations of the earth are shaken.'

I don't read much Scripture at a time, but it informs and impacts me and God spoke to me very specifically through these verses. 'How long will your thinking be so different from mine? How long will you do things back to front? How long, Philippa, will you defend those who are quite able to defend themselves – and let those who cannot go undefended? How long will you invest time in those who don't need your help? How long will you speak for those who are perfectly eloquent? Use your gifts to speak out for those who cannot speak for themselves.'

'Maintain the rights of the poor and oppressed! Speak out for those who have no voices!' I understood once again that God's heart for the poor wasn't just for places like Hong Kong, but that he commanded his people to take positive action to help wherever they might be and whatever form that poverty might take. It might be physical destitution, as in Jesus' story of the rich man and Lazarus, or poverty of spirit, as with the broken-hearted of Isaiah 61. The fatherless whose cause we are commanded to defend could be destitute orphans in a third world country or those whose rich fathers had abused them.

So who are the poor in England? Where are those stuck in dark places? The situation differs from Hong Kong in that few in England are utterly destitute. The Welfare State ensures that orphans receive care. The homeless can apply for housing benefit. Even addicts and alcoholics have somewhere to go. At first sight people here don't seem poor enough.

Bedford is an ordinary town, not especially renowned for its unemployment or homelessness, yet we didn't have to look very hard before finding disadvantaged people hanging around in its centre. In the street where we lived until recently the poor were less obvious, yet we realised that, in the block of four houses which included ours, two widows lived alone. Single mothers, the elderly, the disabled and those with mental problems exist in every community, yet many of us fail to notice them.

God warned the lukewarm church in Laodicea: 'You say, "I am rich; I have acquired wealth and do not need a thing." But you do not realise that you are wretched, pitiful, poor, blind and naked. I counsel you to buy from me gold refined in the fire, so that you can become rich; and white clothes to wear, so that you can cover your shameful nakedness; and salve to put on your eyes, so that you can see' (Revelation 3:17–18).

Christians often tell me they aren't in touch with the poor and I'll reply, 'Think of those who haunt the fringes of our churches – the lonely, the sick, the disabled, those with hidden eating disorders, those who don't feel loved, those who are going nowhere!' We didn't need a Waterloo Bridge: we started with the six contacts we had already. Once your eyes are opened it's not difficult to find damaged and hurting people.

With many we know, from single mothers to single older men, their poverty of spirit far exceeds their material poverty. Sexual abuse victims and people with eating disorders live in their own dark prisons. Addictions and sin keep men and women captive. I pray for myself, and for those working with me, that God would give us salve to put on our eyes, so that we might see with his compassion.

Having seen we can't escape. Jesus taught his disciples to care for the poor in the same way that he did. Scripture commands the church not only to care for one another but to care for the poor – and to act as salt and light in society. 'I was hungry and you gave me something to eat, I was thirsty and you gave me something to drink, I was a stranger and you invited me in, I needed clothes and you clothed me, I was sick and you looked after me, I was in prison and you came to visit me' (Matthew 25:35–36). Clearly Jesus was not afraid to be associated with such people! This thing is not optional. You can't escape the fact that God tells his people throughout the Bible to help the poor. His heart for them permeates the whole of Scripture.

The good news is that, through Jesus, the dead can find life in all its fullness, the guilty can be forgiven, the dirty cleansed, the captives set free and the rejected reconciled. Those in pain can be healed, the grieving can find comfort and even gladness, the despairing praise and the exiled can be integrated into the family of God.

Back in 1989, I knew that we needed to press forward, keeping faith in those promises and trusting God to help us to see them come to pass in Bedford. But then, almost by accident, something happened which was to alter the direction in which we were going and bring us to the brink of disaster.

4

Overwhelmed!

The next sequence of events makes no logical sense. Jenny went off to look for accommodation for herself, Liz and Karen. She reported back that she had found a seven-bedroom house in Clarendon Street for £650 a month. Even by Bedford's standards in 1989, that seemed a ridiculously low rent. After discussion with the Woodside elders, we decided to use it to accommodate both my staff and David's new Frontier Evangelism Team. So far, so good! Then one morning I received a phone call from the elder in charge of finance.

'Philippa, would you like me to cost in one or two bed spaces so that your contacts could have somewhere to sleep in an emergency?' he asked.

'Um … yes, why not?' I replied, my mind half on wedding dresses and guest list. I didn't stop to consider how this might drag us into the residential work which had made me so weary in Macau. So that was how the Clarendon Street Project began really – by 'accident'!

We started renting 50 Clarendon Street in September 1989. Even now, ten years later, as September brings an autumnal sharpness to the air, the memories return and,

as the leaves start falling, a horrid feeling grips my
stomach.

I had to steel myself to take on officialdom, from
seeking planning permission to implementing fire regulations. I had no idea how much all this would cost or
how long it would take. Then a guy called Steve phoned
to say he'd heard that we were opening a drug withdrawal house in Bedford. Could he assist? With the
sensitivity of a brick he turned up half an hour after we
arrived back from honeymoon, to 'help us open our
wedding presents'! It turned out he was an addict, but
despite numerous confrontations he still thought of
himself as a 'staff member' for all of the two years he
stayed in Clarendon Street.

I'd still found no opportunity for staff team training
and I kept being called to church staff meetings in any
overlap time we did have. And then an NFI church from
Newcastle phoned. Would we take in a drug addict?
Foolishly we agreed and a girl with severe, long-term
problems appeared.

Ill-prepared, with no medical cover and an untrained
staff who had never seen me take people off drugs, we
had no chance, really. The girl ran away after forty-eight
hours and we never saw her again. That left my staff dis-
heartened. They'd not worked with me before, nor had
time to establish a relationship of trust.

We started regular Friday night outreach meetings
that October, and soon forty or so needy people
crammed the kitchen at Clarendon Street – sprawled on
the work surfaces, anywhere. Many were drunk, but
they'd come to meet with God. We'd worship, do some
teaching and pray for them. It proved an exciting place

to be because God showed up. Amazing things happened – healings, people repenting under the power of God, words of knowledge. We overheard one guy saying to another, 'Don't let them pray for you, *they know things!*' I'll write more about those meetings in Chapter 8, but one of the great things they did was to provide us with a huge pool of needy people with whom we could work – people whose lives God was touching.

One contact had been one of the biggest drug pushers in town. Others had abused drugs or alcohol for so long that they had become physical and emotional wrecks. Violence, often stemming from drink or uncontrolled anger, formed a natural part of their lives and one of them hinted at murders in the past. Many had problems just as severe – the most severe we've come across in the history of the project – while we had dangerously little experience. I'd worked with violent and broken men in Hong Kong, but this was England, with a different culture, different laws and different support structures. The foundations of what we were trying to do had yet to be established and proved.

We realised though that men like these needed not only somewhere safe and warm to live, but also a refuge where they could separate themselves from their former associates and lifestyle. In other words we needed a Discipleship House, not unlike the ones I'd known in Hong Kong. Where better than Clarendon Street, we thought?

The residential programme started properly in February 1990. Jenny, by faith, went full time the same day that we took in two needy people to disciple – Gail and James. Looking back, James had little intention of changing, but Gail, whose story I'll tell later in more detail, is now happily married with two children and is a leader within the project. Then she was going through real problems. Having suffered abuse, she had developed severe bulimia and regularly slashed her arms with razor blades or broken glass. She'd make progress, but every time I went on holiday there would be another crisis and she'd run away. Jackie Pullinger had taught me not to be afraid to lose someone. It could be the best thing for them, to run off, get knocked around and discover that their former lifestyle wasn't so attractive after all. Though we knew that many would come back again, it didn't stop us worrying.

Newly married, I wasn't around at night, when crises often erupted from nowhere. Karen, Liz and Jenny had to bear the brunt. Not knowing me very well, they didn't realise I'd come if they called.

Others arrived to join them, like Martin, our first male member of staff (apart from the addict, Steve) and Sue. Sue had done a year abroad with YWAM (Youth With A Mission) and returned to England intent on enrolling in their counselling school. However, the secretary of her church back home in Harrow knew that she wanted to work with the poor, with drug addicts and alcoholics on the streets. She told Sue about our work in Bedford and promptly arranged for her to visit us. This was September 1989, when we had just got the house.

Poor Sue found herself plunged into the thick of the action even while I was still showing her round – an enormous resident started head-butting a filing cabinet in the office! That same day she helped me do a Bible study with two of the guys, then to pray with a girl who had just slashed her wrists. We were amazed when she wanted to return, but she said we were doing what she had always wanted to do. After three months she went off on her YWAM course as planned, but was soon back, having chosen us as her field assignment. That was supposed to last for two-and-a-half months, but Sue stayed working on the project for two-and-a-half years!

Meanwhile David's new team who came to live in the house were great, but young and immature, with no real understanding of the work we were trying to do. After a hard day's evangelism they would go down to the pub to relax, yet many of our residents had a problem with alcohol.

We kept taking in people – Matt, for example. Typical of an alcoholic, he'd live in the house for a while, then try to go it alone. During one of these periods he knocked at Clarendon Street's door one night and Jackie Campbell, one of the staff, answered it. Jackie, the daughter of a Woodside Church member, felt called to work with the poor and she proved an enormous strength to us at a very difficult time.

Matt said he'd taken an overdose and, being a nurse, Jackie realised at once that his bright yellow colour meant serious jaundice. She called an ambulance. The hospital said Matt's liver and kidneys had stopped working and gave him twenty-four hours to live. They'd phoned a London hospital but, with Matt's history, they said, what was the point of doing a transplant, even if organs became available?

The hospital did their best to make Matt comfortable. Martin, Jackie and Jenny visited and prayed with him, but nothing dramatic happened. After they returned to

Clarendon Street the phone rang. It was Matt's consultant, a Hindu. 'I don't understand this,' he said. 'Everything has started working – it's as though Matt's been born again!'

The residents did incredibly well, but to be catapulted off the streets into live-in Christian discipleship was a huge jump for them. It worked for one or two, but most found the change hard to sustain. Though removed from their former worlds, they had not yet been cut off from them. Some did show a soft side which amazed us, knowing the horrific acts which they had committed, but they had no time to adjust, to grow in their new-found faith. Often they ran away, though most returned again later. Matt ended up in London one time, drinking in a Soho bar, when a man offered to buy him a drink.

Streetwise Matt wasn't sure. 'Yeah, but don't try anything!' he warned.

'It's OK,' said the stranger, 'I'm a Christian. God told me your name is Matt and I'm to give you £20. I thought you'd only spend it on drink but God said he won't let you do that. You're to use it for your train fare to Bedford. Er … do you know anyone in Bedford, Matt?'

Matt came back, sobered in all respects!

Meanwhile I was beginning to train the staff and found that I loved to reproduce ministry in this way. I also loved trouble-shooting and problem-solving – up to a point. We never knew what would happen next and felt unprepared for most of it. Every time David and I tried to get away for a much-needed break, something would happen. Once an old alcoholic called Badger phoned us at home, so drunk he didn't know what he was doing. I guess he thought he'd put the phone down but he hadn't.

We could hear a kind of droning singing and didn't feel we could leave until we'd resolved the situation ... but with our phone still busy we couldn't ring the others and so had to deal with it ourselves.

Another time we were about to set off when Clarendon Street phoned to say that one of the residents was eating their front wall – actually chewing the cement of the gatepost. Colin, six foot five and big with it, was fine if sober, but on one of his 'hyper-benders' of drink and drugs he would become amazingly energised, threatening and abusive. He locked me in a room with him once, and didn't like it when I tried to retrieve the knife from his sock. He grabbed my arm and wouldn't let go, though to be fair he damaged himself rather than me.

We first met him when he knocked on Clarendon Street's door, asking for a cup of coffee. We invited him in and explained the good news about Jesus.

'That's amazing!' he said. 'Why's no one told me about this before?' Opening right up, he admitted to having been suicidal. 'But that helpline never told me any of this Jesus stuff,' he complained.

We had been offering him the possibility of living in the house for a few months before he announced, 'I'm ready to follow God now!' and moved in. He really had met with God and his life began to improve. Despite his alcoholism he found a steady girlfriend and a job and was developing self-respect, until his girlfriend chucked him. He started drinking again and lost his job. Colin isn't in a good place now, though he still turns up at our Friday night outreach from time to time.

Back to the famous occasion when he ate the wall: he'd got angry with one of the staff, then raced outside and up and down the school playing fields nearby, shouting, 'Liar, liar!' As the neighbours turned out to watch, he started chucking wheelie bins around the street. These days we'd have called the police but the staff merely dodged the bins and tried to calm him down, while one of them phoned me. Then they heard his teeth crunching on the gatepost – you can still see the marks he made. On another occasion he sank his teeth into a neighbour's wall in our road, knocking it down. Afterwards he ran off and one of the staff retrieved him in her car – only to be reported for dangerous driving by someone who thought it was she who had damaged the wall!

Some incidents seem hilarious, looking back, though I don't remember laughing much myself in those early days. Colin phoned at two in the morning from the police station when a girl called Emma was leading the house. He'd been on a binge and failed to return to Clarendon Street. Then he'd broken into the police station where he was phoning from one of the offices.

'Can you come and pick me up, Emma?' he asked. 'Go round the back and call my name. Quiet, mind!'

Emma and a male staff member set off in a spirit of adventure. They called, 'Colin! Colin!' in stage whispers all round the back of the police station. When nothing happened they returned to the hostel. A few hours later Colin turned up on the doorstep, still very drunk. Like a conspirator he whispered, 'Look what I've got!' When he produced a policeman's helmet and a pad of incident report forms, the staff calmed him down and told him he would have to take them back in the morning.

The next day, when they drove him to the police station, Colin seemed reluctant to confess at the desk and so they compromised. Waiting until everyone was occupied, Colin managed to nip past and dump his trophies in an interview room. Somewhat unorthodox, but then with no real training or experience, my staff had no idea of the proper course of action in such circumstances!

Everyday life proved chaotic. Disturbed residents often tried to damage or kill themselves, which is why we took all the locks off the toilet doors. (Live-in staff learnt to sing or pray loudly, or else developed bowel problems!) One night a female resident with psychiatric problems set herself alight in the garden. Emma and a couple of other female helpers managed to put out the flames and to get her back into the kitchen, where she started kicking the vegetable rack and throwing tables and chairs about. The whole house came running as the three of them tried to restrain her.

In those days this kind of incident drew all the staff in, and wore everyone out! Now we would assign two specific individuals to deal with it, and life in the rest of the house continues as normal.

We tried to provide some structure for the residents' days, though little things like persuading them to get up in the morning often turned into major confrontations. First we had them tidying up the garden at Clarendon Street, and later took them to a Christian conference centre nearby for some art and horticulture, which could all too easily descend into chaos.

We made so many mistakes, partly because I was demanding 110 per cent commitment from the live-in staff. Lacking not only understanding but common ideals and support, they were unprepared for dealing with the disturbed, violent or plain difficult people who came to us. Lurching from crisis to crisis, steeling themselves to face yet another dangerous situation, it was no wonder they didn't feel safe! Nor could they get away, since most lived on the project.

Live-in conditions didn't help. The bedrooms and corridors smelt of damp, mould flourished and we had to pray in money for rubbish bins, light bulbs and other basic commodities. When a £300 electricity bill arrived, it caused panic, especially when we realised that it would be followed, in three months, by another.

I hadn't even thought to schedule lunch breaks into staff timetables, while emergencies or staff sickness meant their one evening or day off a week got cancelled, as often as not. Stress and overwork combined to make many fall ill. They saw me returning to my husband at the end of the evening, just when things were getting difficult. Then, having stayed up all night, they faced their paid jobs the next day.

Not surprisingly, staff morale hit an all-time low. The only way from there was up and we did learn from our mistakes. I'm writing this not to discourage anyone from working with the poor, but in the hope that others can benefit from our experience and avoid rock-bottom. From bitter experience, these are the factors which demotivate workers and helpers:

• Leadership lacks clarity and strategy.
• The person empowered to make decisions is absent when decisions need to be taken.

- No one knows what they are supposed to be doing, so that everyone feels responsible for everything.
- Workers receive insufficient support and training.
- Conflicts remain unresolved.
- Staff lack the basic requirements for life – shelter, food, clothing, sleeping conditions, washing facilities, time off.
- There are no opportunities for developing friendships or male/female relationships.
- Staff have poor salaries and career development and no pension – that may be fine for a year or two, but people are unlikely to stay long-term.

For my part, though I lived away from Clarendon Street, as leader I found the responsibility hard to bear. The stakes, the risks we were taking, climbed higher and higher. The more staff and residents were involved, the more lives could be damaged. Away from Clarendon Street, when I tried to apply a little objectivity I saw things going from bad to worse and felt overwhelmed at the enormity of the task ahead. Occasionally I'd be in tears over the breakfast table, saying to David, 'I'm not sure I can do this today.' Not one to give in easily, I nevertheless found myself admitting to Dave Devenish, 'I don't think I can pull this off.' The finances weren't working. I felt trapped and the project seemed dangerously unstable. But we carried on.

That's not to say that good things didn't happen. We saw people coming off drugs, painlessly – proving the power of prayer. I'd not really doubted that God would be faithful in that respect – I'd seen it too often in Hong Kong – but I knew also that miracles didn't guarantee that someone would change. That had always proved far more problematic, with steps forward and then back, depending on whether the person made good or bad decisions. My expectations were more realistic than those of the church, many of whom seemed to expect people to come off the streets one day, find Jesus the next and turn into model disciples by the end of the week.

We did see miracles, though – miracles of protection when we had no idea of how to keep people safe. When the two large hostels next door were bought up and converted to private houses again, a former street guy vented his anger by setting fire to them. The fire burnt right up to our wall – and stopped. One of the staff had a vision of two angels with swords guarding the door of 50 Clarendon Street. Then, shortly afterwards, a huge, dangerous guy we knew came looking for a resident, wanting to beat him up. Each time he tried to get into the house, he bounced off some invisible shield, then hurled himself forward in anger again, only to bounce back harder. In the end he gave up and slunk off in disgust.

Another time two staff members on duty at night saw a fine haze filling the ground floor of the house. Convinced that someone was smoking dope, they searched the place but found nothing. It occurred to one of them that it might be the presence of God. On suggesting this he crashed out on the floor. The other found himself able to do nothing but intercede and cry out to God all night for revival.

Meanwhile our Friday night meetings and street work brought in yet more contacts who wanted to know about Jesus and whether he really could make a difference to their lives …

5

Defining a Vision

When I started, I dreamt of seeing the changes described in Isaiah 61 happen among the poor in Bedford, but I couldn't have told you how. The local church had given me a job to do: to care for and disciple the most difficult contacts which David and his team were making on the estate. I responded to their needs and to those of others I met. Willing to pray and work all hours, I was ready to keep loving them way beyond the point of hurting. I disciplined myself to keep my own actions and attitudes consistent and godly, to show there was another way of living. In fact, apart from residential work – I'd had enough of that in Hong Kong – I was ready to do anything.

But I never sat down and thought, 'What, specifically, is God asking me to do? What is the vision he's giving me?' I knew he was asking me to interpret Isaiah 61 but I needed something more concrete than that. I never asked who exactly we should help. In Hong Kong that had been clear – we worked with addicts – but the people drawn to us in Bedford expressed every type of poverty from mental illness and eating disorders to abuse, rejection, violence and prostitution. I can think of so many questions now. Did we have the skills and the facilities which we needed to meet all these needs? If not, which should we tackle first? What structure could we use? How would we set about acquiring training, buildings, equipment, staff or anything else that was necessary? At the time none of this occurred to me.

If I see someone hurting, I'm the kind of person who will respond by trying to do something to help. I believe, passionately, that God longs to bring justice or healing or whatever the situation requires, so to me it's obvious that if Christians bring good news into that situation, it will improve. If I see a problem, I'll see a solution – and go for it with tenacity. That means, more often than not, things happen. But I struggled to equip others to help me in this task because I never was any good at sharing my vision, partly because I didn't understand properly what it was and partly because I didn't know how to articulate it. I've always been a do-er and a listener, not a talker.

I'd never sat down with the church leaders and thought through our priorities – what we were trying to achieve and what we would need to put in place in order to achieve it. So we had no shape, no structure, just growing numbers of people whose acute problems demanded our attention day and night. We responded to those problems out of good hearts, but failed to be proactive or to provide a sense of direction.

What had begun as a snowball of needs turned into an avalanche. As it thundered around us, we risked not only letting down the damaged people we were trying to help but wrecking our own lives and relationships – and our church – along with them. I had a lot to learn about leadership and how to establish an effective ministry.

In fact, we've found that the main key to establishing a ministry is to identify and develop leadership. That in itself throws up many issues which are absolutely vital to resolve before ministry can be undertaken, so I want to spend some time examining some of these issues.

A common mistake is to assume that, because a church is good-hearted and well-disposed towards the poor, it is time to start a ministry with them. But unless you have the right leader for that ministry, it is not yet necessarily time. Without a clear leader, the church will end up with as many ministries with the poor as it has people. When nothing effective is established everyone will conclude that ministering to the poor doesn't work.

So let's take a look at some of the 'how-tos' of setting up a ministry with the poor, starting with the most fundamental.

What makes a leader?

I've found that four main issues of character and gifting determine whether or not someone becomes a godly leader:

A determination to face reality in faith, no matter what

When you invest your life in building something it's easy to overlook its weaknesses, yet leaders need the ability to detach themselves and see their ministry with the ruthless honesty of an outsider. Only then can one make appropriate adjustments. For example, when things went wrong later with one of our houses I had to say, 'Look, this place is in a real state. The building's revolting, the staff aren't motivated and no one knows what they are supposed to be doing. In fact it's dangerous and I wouldn't want to live or work here. So let's overhaul it, changing everything if necessary.' That was a hard thing to do, because I had created the place and remained responsible for it.

Admitting that things had gone badly wrong could have proved disastrous, unless I had maintained faith – faith in the vision, faith in the people involved in it and faith in God. Over the years I've had to face many residents and staff with issues in their lives which needed changing. That kind of truth hurts, which is why I knew it was important to communicate faith – faith that change was possible. I made it very clear that I would support them through the process of change, no matter what. Soon they not only wanted to change but believed that it was possible too. A leader who faces reality in faith will see change happen!

The ability to make things happen

These days people come to the project saying that they have a vision for their own work. They come and visit, spend time on team training and go away, yet we never hear of anything that they have established later. Why is that? Nine times out of ten it is because they do not have the catalytic ability to translate what is in their heart into reality. They lack the ability to make things happen, to light fires, to start things from scratch. Not all leaders have this ability, but for those who do, it can be sharpened. How? Reading management training books helps but the main way is by working alongside other good leaders on a clear delegation scale. Good leaders give both opportunities and support and make their trainees accountable for productivity.

Faithfulness and endurance

It is not always the most vocal, ambitious or charismatic individual who will establish a real work of God. Some impressive-seeming people have come on our project's staff, but in three or four months have burnt out and gone on to something else. I've learnt to look for the plodders rather than the sprinters; for those who make good decisions and establish a track record of faithfulness. Ultimately, the person who is there at both the beginning and the end is the person who will establish and lead a work successfully.

An ability to be proactive rather than reactive

Who, or what, will shape your ministry? Is it circumstances? Or the pressure of others' opinion? Or your own vision? It is important to learn from others and to take the opportunities which circumstances offer, but if you are going to build what God has called you to build, then you will need to plan your vision and make it work. Our first house in the project came about by 'accident', but the second resulted from me having a vision which I pressed to see fulfilled. If I had waited for circumstances nothing would have happened, and it was the same when we came to start our third and fourth houses. There are times when leaders must pursue their vision aggressively, provided it is in a right attitude to godly authority.

Shaping your vision

Looking back, only God's grace saved us from disaster. He started shaping my vision by introducing the very thing I'd tried to avoid. He slipped in residential work while I wasn't looking and the problems it brought threatened to overwhelm us.

Jenny kept asking me: 'Where are we going with this, Philippa? Where do you expect to be in three months? What is your vision?'

I felt confused by her questioning. I was seeking to obey God! Our aim was to see Isaiah 61 fulfilled. What was this vision business?

When I realised that I needed help to tease out more detail, I sat down with Dave Devenish, who led our church at the time. He asked me a series of questions.

'Is this project meant to be big or little, Philippa?'

I hesitated. 'Both.'

'What do you mean by that?'

'Well, it's not to be big in the sense of institutional but it will affect lots of people.'

'OK, if you say it doesn't feel institutional, what does it feel like?'

'Like family. There'll be lots of small, family units, not one huge thing.'

'So you're looking at lots of houses. Will they all be the same?'

'No, they'll differ according to the needs of the people in them.'

'What about the staff? You'll need to build a team. What kind of person are you looking for?'

'Not one kind of person, certainly not one type or personality. But they would be the same in that each of them would long to see lives changed through the power of the gospel.'

'Would they be ordinary people or ones with special training or skill?'

'Ordinary – but God would use them to do extraordinary things!'

Dave continued to ask me questions until finally he said, 'Philippa, you do have a vision – and a specific one. You've answered all of my questions in great detail. You know what you have seen. I believe you know what God is asking of you now.'

Yes I did, I realised, though it had taken Dave's questioning for me to articulate it fully, even in my own mind.

Do you have a vision?

When the problems at the Hostel threatened to overwhelm all of us and bring the whole project crashing down, I prayed and sought God. He did speak further to me in the end, giving me a clear sense of the shape of the vision. At the same time he spoke to me about training others.

In the course of doing so, I've met many young people with great potential for leadership who have similar problems in articulating their vision. I'm aware that, at the end of their time with us, if they go away to establish a vague vision, either nothing will happen or they will end up in as bad a mess as we did. That's why I want to write here some questions which you could ask yourself, should God be stirring up a vision within you. It will take time, work, prayer and conversation to do this properly. I would suggest that you not only write down the answers but also talk them over with a friend or church leader. It could prove messy, but then what baby is born without both mess and pain?

A vision is:

- Something God has put into us, which will be in line with our gifting.
- Something we long to see happen through us in our lifetime.
- Something we believe in and would fight for – not someone else's good idea.
- Something we will bring to birth and establish ourselves, or which we contribute towards (for example by serving on its leadership team).

The majority of people will be called by God to serve the visions of one or more others. Their work is every bit as important as that of the leaders, but normally God gives a vision to the leader whom he calls to bring it to birth.

So, I ask aspiring leaders who have come to work on our project: Do you have a vision? A few will have looked at their visions full on. They will already have asked God, and themselves, the questions which I was so slow to ask. Some may have a growing sense of what that vision is and when it might begin – be that two years or twenty down the line. Others may have glimpsed something out of the corner of their eye and found it so terrifying that they ran away. I've known plenty who shrank from examining their visions because of inverted pride. 'Who do I think I am, even beginning to wonder if I could do this?' or 'What on earth would people think of me? It sounds so arrogant to even mention the possibility!'

There's no doubt that visions need testing, or that a friend's wise advice can prove humbling. Potential leaders need to brace themselves for these two processes because the fact is, a vision has to be spoken out before we really connect with it ourselves. It has to be spoken out before we get on and do anything about it and certainly before we recruit others to follow us in it.

Articulating your vision

In our training programme we've found it helpful to ask potential leaders to articulate their vision first of all in broad terms, by asking them to complete the following sentence: *My life will be complete if, before I die* ....

So what would you put? There is no right or wrong answer. This is about finding out what God has put in you as an individual.

One of my staff wrote, 'My life will be complete if, before I die, I have:

1. seen Bedford change through the removal of homelessness;
2. worked to see Christian churches in England equipped to care for the poor;
3. lived in India and established a work that cares for homeless street children.'

Once you have seen what your long-term vision is you will be better equipped to order your life and priorities accordingly. You will also begin to be able to communicate it to those who, by following you, will help bring it to pass.

The next stage is to hone it down. Most people on our courses are in their twenties, so we ask them to write down what they would like to see happen by the time they are forty. But for you, however old or young you are, wrestle with God over this question, then ask yourself: *What would I like to see accomplished through me within the next ten or fifteen years?*

Don't be afraid of seeking God about your aims in this way. It's important because if you aim at nothing, you're likely to hit nothing! I don't believe God normally shows people everything which they may accomplish, nor detailed plans, month by month, of what will happen. And the visions we do have may be adjusted or reinterpreted through life's changes. If we have a clear idea of the direction in which we are heading, it may strengthen us for the period of preparation God takes us through in order to clarify our vision.

You see, though I believe he takes ordinary people and turns them into leaders with vision, they can't stay ordinary. We now have four hostels in Bedford, but even a project as insignificant as ours wasn't brought to birth by ordinary people. Establishing it took us into extreme lifestyles, where we were giving every ounce of energy and doing our utmost to walk in devotion with God.

When I hear people say that their vision is to affect nations, I wonder: What will their days look like? What kind of teams will they need to build? What kind of daily walk with Christ will they have? What about fasting and silence, intimacy, sacrifice …?

We need to let God form that which he has placed within us so that it becomes useful in his kingdom. Ask him for specifics: What life do you want me to lead? What sacrifices are you calling me to? How are you wanting to shape and fashion my life? If you see his hand on you and know his vision burning within you, it is easier to embrace the lessons he is teaching you.

Once you have written down the answers to these questions, talk about them with trustworthy Christians who will not be afraid to hold you to them. They will spur you on when things get tough or when you start wondering whether you imagined God's calling in the first place.

Honing your vision – fleshing out the detail

The next stage is to become even more specific. Maybe you've been through a period of training and God is saying, 'Your ministry will begin soon.' I thought Hong Kong was my period of training and so plunged straight into the work in Bedford without understanding the specifics of my vision. I wouldn't recommend that route! For one thing, when you are leading a team the others need to know what they are buying into, where they are going, what the priorities and value systems will be and what the thing is supposed to feel like. Even so, your vision won't emerge fully fledged and you may be in for a bumpy ride at first, but if you're all aiming for the same thing, you are far more likely to avoid a fatal crash landing.

People often find it helpful at this stage to ask themselves lots of questions, or to get a friend to ask them, as

Dave Devenish did for me. If you push yourself for the answers or encourage your friend to corner you, you may be surprised at how much emerges!

Here are examples of the kind of questions you could ask:

- Could I draw my vision?
- How big or small is it?
- How many people are in it?
- What kind of people group? Do they like me? Am I gifted with them?
- What exactly do I want to do, e.g. soup kitchen, counselling, prison work, residential?
- What are the workers like?
- Where is it geographically? On the streets or in a house?
- What will I need, not only for the 'ministry' but for admin, training, team meetings, etc?
- When is it? Day or night? Is it to happen soon or in the medium-term?
- What does it feel like?
- Do I see myself doing this alongside other paid employment or full time?
- What will my days look like?
- What will I have to give up to make this happen?
- What is driving me to do this? (That is what you will use to motivate others!)
- What has God put in me as a person which makes me want to do this?
- Why would others want to come and join me?
- If this project is to be part of a larger team or church, how will we work together?

- Who will oversee this?
- Where will the finance come from?

Can you write your vision in one sentence? When the Salvation Army said that they wanted to make citizens out of the rejected, everyone knew exactly what they were about – and that's powerful. We said that we were providing 'a safe place for the broken'. If you don't understand your vision so well that you can write it down in one sentence, perhaps you need to seek God again and ask more questions.

Next write your vision in three sentences and finally in twenty. This will help you to communicate it to others both in essence and in some detail. Try to avoid religious jargon. Don't say, 'My vision is to set the captives free.' Make it practical, e.g. 'My vision is to have a project that models excellence, values the poor and trains the workers so that they are able to go and establish other projects. It will be a model for other churches, because it's been worked through ordinary people whose lives are becoming more like Jesus in the process.'

My vision in one sentence is ....

My vision in three sentences is:
  1.
  2.
  3.

My vision in twenty sentences is:
  1.
  2.

3.
4.
5.
6.
7.
8.
9.
10.
11.
12.
13.
14.
15.
16.
17.
18.
19.
20.

There is plenty more work to be done on practical planning – on turning your honed vision into reality – but we'll look at that in the next chapter.

6

Laying Good Foundations

In February 1990, five months after we obtained the house in Clarendon Street, I had reached exasperation point. As we lurched from crisis to crisis I could see no way to stabilise matters. Sensing the staff's unease, I questioned my own ability to build a team and worried that I'd brought them here under false pretences. I thought I'd clarified my vision but now became unsure again of what I was supposed to be doing. I started wondering if I'd misheard God from the beginning. Did he want me involved with the poor at all, or had my Hong Kong enthusiasm carried me outside his will? Should I close the whole project down?

David, seeing something of this soul-searching, said to me one day, 'Look, you need to settle this. Your indecision about whether the project should exist or not is paralysing everything.' It was true. Unless I heard from God one way or the other I wouldn't be able to move forward or address any of the issues. David and I set aside an evening to pray together. 'And we'll keep going until God speaks,' David said.

Ten minutes after we started, as clear as anything,

God said to me, 'Luke 7.' Looking the passage up in the Bible I read about how John the Baptist, in prison, sent his disciples to ask Jesus if he were God's Anointed One, or if they were to wait for another.

Jesus didn't reply directly to their question but said, 'Go and tell John what you have seen and heard: the blind receive their sight, the lame walk, the lepers are cleansed, the deaf hear, the dead are raised and the poor have good news preached to them.'

I had been asking whether Jesus was in the project or not. Now I realised that these things are always a sign of his presence. I felt him say to me, 'Just get on and do it,' and those words, combined with Scripture, restored my confidence.

Though he had confirmed my vision, that didn't help me find a way to tame the chaos of our daily struggle, so I took to walking and praying for an hour a day on a nearby golf course. Keeping this up, day after day for nearly a year, I must have walked miles, but God kept silent. To me it felt like hard labour, an act of sheer obedience. Then one day in January 1991, it was as though heaven opened for about ten minutes and God spoke, as simply and clearly as he had said 'Luke 7': 'There are to be four houses in Bedford: the first a night shelter, a place where those who are unable to hold down accommodation can be housed, fed, clothed and cared for; the second a hostel, a safe place to house those who don't know Jesus – the alcoholic, the addict, the abused, the manic depressive; the third a discipleship house where the same people, having come to know Jesus, can sort out their lives; and the fourth a halfway house back into the community – a place where individuals can live in a small, safe environment and learn the basic skills of looking after a home for themselves.'

That was all. His blueprint never came again with such clarity, yet it sounded so 'normal' I could have missed it. But that was all I needed. Now I knew what I had to do, I could put things in place to make it happen.

He said one more sentence. 'You are to break down everything that comes naturally to you and give it away.' He was speaking of training, which became my top priority.

From the simple words about the first house, I understood how someone could come off the streets to the Night Shelter, using it for as long or as short a time as necessary. After all, God loves the poor whether or not they become Christians. Now we could care for those on the streets without plunging them straight into intense discipleship. We could offer unconditional love rather than saying, 'We'll give you a home but you'll have to follow Jesus first.' The person wouldn't have to be a Christian, not even to go on to the less transitory environment of the Hostel.

At the Hostel he (or she) could learn to sort out his chaotic lifestyle a bit but, if he hit difficulties, could always return to the less demanding Night Shelter for a while. If, on the other hand, he progressed well, he might leave the Hostel having found work and accommodation of his own.

Those finding Jesus might eventually become ready to live in the third stage Discipleship House (our previous entry point). There they could grow in their faith and sort out more issues in their lives. Finally, some people would need a smaller halfway house to practise life skills, such as how to cook or to budget money, before they ventured to live independently. Someone might work through all four stages of our houses, going forwards or backwards between them as necessary. Others might use one only – maybe the Night Shelter. Christians whose lives had become a mess because they had missed out on working through foundational issues, or because they'd been damaged through falling into serious sin, might enter the Discipleship House and use only that.

With the blueprint clear in my mind I could begin to formulate an action plan. I knew that I had to lay the right foundations for the project, which God intended to grow far larger than anything I had imagined before. Up to now our residential work had developed by accident. Now I could learn from our past mistakes, establish ground rules, share vision, train the staff and equip the project for the long haul. I knew it would take years. The houses would be established one at a time. We had started back to front with the third stage, the Discipleship House. Having been set up in a haphazard fashion it would need to change greatly, but I didn't mind all the work now that I had hope and real vision again – now I could see how it would work.

I also had two full-time workers for the first time. A friend from my old church phoned saying she had six months spare before starting a course. Could she come and help? Although we had no money, we took the step of faith of bringing Jenny on board full time too. That is to say we paid her rent and food bills and gave her £10 a month pocket money!

I set about planning how to develop Clarendon Street from its former haphazard collection of uses to become a house dedicated to residential discipleship. We needed to tackle it on all levels. Physically we set about conquering the damp, little by little, then redecorated the rooms and improved the feel of the place.

We arranged for David's evangelistic team to move out one by one. To have lost all their rent money in one go would have ruined our cash flow. Meanwhile, I thought hard about the ground rules needed to ensure the smooth running of such a venture, long-term. For the safety of everyone we had to decide what behaviour we could tolerate and what sanctions we would apply should people overstep the limits. For the staff too we needed sensible regulations – proper timetables, for one thing, including lunch breaks! We needed enough slack in the timetable to cover sickness and holidays and so guarantee days off. All of this didn't happen overnight, but we began a steep learning curve and slowly things started to improve.

Turning your vision into a reality

I have met many people who say they want to establish projects, yet despite their obvious leadership gifts and what sounds like specific, God-given vision, nothing ever happens. One problem is that if you are leading something into being, no one will spur you on, checking, 'Have you done this or that?' Important things get left. A nagging voice questions, 'Who do you think you are, starting something like this in your twenties?' or asks, 'Did God really tell you to do this?'

It's easy to think, 'I'm young and inexperienced. In another twenty years, I'll be better equipped to lead this thing.' That may be true, but I have to ask: Where are all the forty-somethings starting projects? It's most often the young and inexperienced who bring the necessary vision and energy, have less to leave behind and more time in which to work things out. But a little training and strategy helps no end!

At this stage of establishing the four-fold project I had to work hard on the detail. Despite God giving me his clear blueprint of vision, nothing would have happened if I'd not sat down, brainstormed, prioritised, made lists of what needed doing month by month and worked my way through them systematically. Maybe there are other ways to plan, strategise and make things happen, but I haven't found them. It's all too easy to get caught up with what seems to be urgent – like planning a Bible study for that night's house group – while not making a boring phone call, but the future of your project may ultimately depend on the appointment you make during that mundane or difficult telephone conversation!

As I said, I don't want merely to tell a story in this book but to give some practical help as to how to get things done. So, if any of you has a vision, how do you start? What do you do at nine o'clock in the morning?

Setting priorities

The first three stages would be:

1. Clarify your vision.
2. Prove that you have the ability to work within that area.
3. For a ministry based in a local church, get permission

from your church leadership to start the ministry, and talk through major issues with them to make sure they are in tune with your vision.

I've written about the above elsewhere in this book. Here I want to look in more detail at the next very practical stages of translating a vision into reality.

Brainstorm

Whether I'm planning a training course, writing a book or starting a night shelter, I sit down with a blank piece of paper and jot down anything which I may need to do. At this stage it matters not at all about the order, just write things down as they spring to mind. You might think 'legal implications', for example. Who could you approach? Does your church use a solicitor? Is there one among the church members? Make a note to find out and contact people as appropriate.

You might think 'training needs'. Do you yourself need training, for example in finance, management or counselling? How might you obtain it? Can you visit similar projects elsewhere? How will you find out about them? List phone calls to make. Who will train those who will work alongside you? Are you skilled in training people yourself? If not, who would you trust to do this training – Christian or secular – and would you need to contribute to it alongside them?

Finance. Where will it come from? Find out about and investigate the viability of various sources for both revenue and capital expenditure. To whom will you be accountable, financially?

Staff. How will you recruit them? Jot down any ideas.

Think about interviews and contracts of employment.
There's no point reinventing the wheel. Could other
organisations help you with this kind of thing? Once you
have staff, what do you expect them to do from 9am to
10am and every other hour of the day? Do you need
shifts or rotas? If so, how will they work? How will you
give support and build a team?

What about your contacts or residents? How will
you make your services known among them and gain
their trust? How far do you need to structure the time
they spend on your project? What rules and regulations do you need? What policies must you lay down?
For example do you need to establish policies on violence and abusive language, weapons, HIV, paedophiles or drugs and alcohol on site? What about
male/female relationships on your staff or among residents?

Consider other requirements, like insurance, publicity
and medical cover. Find out about planning permission,
building regulations, fire regulations and food regulations. Investigate hygiene and diet, health and safety and
the implications of legal matters such as employment
law or the Children's Act. Write down all the different
departments you need to contact.

How exactly is your relationship with your local
church going to work? With whom do you need to talk
through issues like where your pastoral support will
come from and who exactly is responsible for what?

I'll write about many of these things in more detail
later. For now, simply brainstorm, and, depending on
the kind of project you want to establish, I'm sure you
will be able to think of many more things to cover.

Expand your brainstorm

For example, under my heading 'We need buildings', I wrote the names of our local housing associations and authorities, and then thought of others such as commercial agents or even the National Health Service which sometimes has 'spare' buildings they may let others use. I worked through my list approaching them all.

As it turned out none of our buildings came this way, but in my experience you have to do something, to start somewhere – and then God will break in and work in his own supernatural, or natural, ways.

Prioritise

When David was church-planting he had these words displayed above his desk: 'The main thing is to keep to the main thing – the main thing!' And that is what you need to do. Put everything in a time schedule. Decide when your project is to start and then work out, month by month, exactly when everything needs doing in order to meet your deadline. Write lists for each month, including anything ongoing which needs to happen every month. Everything on that list is your priority. Once you've crossed everything off for that month, then you can do other things.

I found that my work on establishing the project took about eight mornings a month. Those mornings could seem both boring and difficult as I researched the finer legal points or 'cold-called' local government departments to book appointments to explain what we planned to do. If you want to establish a ministry you will have to work through all this. Personally I don't know of any way of forcing myself to do things I hate other than to work through my priorities in what feels like a series of cold-blooded decisions. That's how a vision becomes reality. If you find yourself side-stepping things you find difficult, tell someone about it and ask them to chase you!

Working with professionals

Christians can live in their own world of visions but anyone taking on a project caring for people will have to learn to work with a whole range of professionals who may not share their beliefs or world view. It's easy for the voluntary sector to lack confidence or to start off on the wrong foot with these people, but there is no need for Christians to do this if we follow certain principles.

Understanding

We must learn to understand the other professionals, and to change our attitude towards them if necessary. The voluntary sector can take various wrong turnings. Some may be overawed by those with a high degree of training, or those carrying governmental authority. Many professional organisations assume that the voluntary sector is unprofessional. We mustn't be intimidated, but in humility keep proving them wrong!

Many Christians write off certain professionals, deciding on limited hearsay evidence that they don't do a proper job. We need to understand the difference in the scope of our work in order to build mutual respect. In the voluntary sector we can choose every resident, every contact, while social services have to deal with everyone, whether or not they have the finances, the training and the expertise. It's all too easy for us to dismiss social services as uncaring because they assess, then dismiss one of our contacts who is crying out for help. We don't take into account that a thousand other people may have approached them with even more serious problems that month. When we come to understand other professionals and the pressures they are under, we will begin to build bridges and to see how our work can complement theirs.

It's true that professionals may differ from us in their approach or in their philosophy of caring. Instead of being tense and uneasy in our relations we need to try to understand and appreciate them, without compromising our own contribution.

Our understanding of counselling is likely to be different and they may not understand why certain things are important to us – like being accountable to church leadership. With the best will in the world, different terminology can confuse communication between us. They may not understand our Christian-speak, so with them I won't talk about a discipleship house but a rehabilitation house, for example.

Knowing when other departments should be involved

Project staff need to be clear at what point they should call in other organisations such as social services, doctors, psychiatrists and the police. The same applies to local authority departments such as housing, environmental health and planning. It's important to know the legal requirements, but there are many grey areas.

Always establish policy by talking things through in a calm way with your church leadership and with the organisations concerned. Then, when a crisis happens, you will know what to do and when to call on other professionals.

(a) Social services What happens if a sixteen-year-old turns up at your night shelter? Or someone younger? You would need to involve social services. We ask every potential resident whether they have a social worker and, if so, we arrange to talk to that person as early as possible.

(b) Health professionals and the environmental health department Does your environmental health policy mention what to do if a resident has scabies? Which illnesses would you report? Is your food preparation as safe as it could be? It's important that you consult your local environmental health department before setting up your project and act on its advice. Afterwards take note of its regular checks and reviews. How might the Health and Safety at Work Act affect your project? What governs the relationship between resident, doctor and carer? Is medical co-operation a condition of residency? We ask residents for the name and address of their GP. When appropriate we seek permission to communicate with the health professionals caring for a person, especially if he or she is undergoing psychiatric care. We also ask for access to decision-making about that person.

(c) Housing department When residents wish to move on, you will need to liaise with the housing depart-

ment, which has a legal obligation to house them if they are homeless. You have to write to the housing department, stating that the person is being asked to leave and will therefore be homeless from such and such a date. That sounds harsh but it is the way the system works.

By establishing good relations with our housing department we have been able to circumvent all kinds of red tape, mainly because it recognises that we provide a service which it too is obliged to provide, and it is grateful. In this way we obtain housing benefit for sixteen- and seventeen-year-olds who are not normally eligible. The forms, which can take half an hour to fill in, are beyond many of our residents' understanding. We have negotiated that they need only sign them as they arrive and we fill in the rest at a convenient moment. Housing benefit is normally payable by the week, which means night shelters lose out as people often stay only a night or two. Our housing department has agreed to pay housing benefit by the night for those in our Shelter.

(d) The police If your staff hear two people joking about abusing someone, or discussing a crime they committed, what action should be taken? The legal position is that the voluntary sector is not obliged to report any crime other than those falling under the Prevention of Terrorism Act, but what is the moral position?

Do you call the police only to protect staff, neighbours and residents from violence, or do you foster more of a relationship with them? Under what circumstances would you press charges against residents or others?

(e) Planning department It is important to find out the planning status of any building you are seeking to rent or buy and to check that the use you intend for it does not contravene its registered status. If it does, then you need to apply to the planning department for a change in the status. Depending on when the planning committee sits, the whole process can take up to six months, from beginning to end.

How to liaise with other professionals

We have found it best to act on policies of maximum information and maximum co-operation, so long as this does not compromise our unique Christian contribution. Occasionally other professionals will say, 'We don't want you praying with this person.' In that case we would reply, 'But we exist to give spiritual support and this person, by coming here, is requiring that care. If you feel that is inappropriate you can tell the person so, but we need to be permitted to support them in the way which we feel is appropriate.' Use their vocabulary. Don't talk about 'when we were praying and worshipping, God said' if you can simply say 'we have decided'.

It is always good to meet other professionals and establish a working relationship with them before any crises develop. As the project is being established, take the initiative and ask for meetings – and in the case of large organisations such as the police or social services, ask for a specific point of contact which you can use again and again. Many of them will have a community relations officer. They will need a point of contact within your organisation too. If they speak to a different person every time they phone, they may have difficulty believing that any action is being taken. That point of contact might be the leader or an appropriate key worker, but if your staff turnover is high, it would be better to make the main point of contact someone relatively senior who will be around for a few years.

It's important to keep scrupulous records of dealings with other professionals. File copies of your letters to them and theirs to you. After a significant telephone conversation or meeting, especially if they have given you advice, write them a letter summarising any important points and keep a copy yourself. Make sure that all your letters are professional, with correct spelling and grammar, enlisting the help of someone else in the church if no one on your team is suitably qualified!

Don't leave detailed messages for other professionals, as you will not know whether or not they have received them.

Keep appointments. These people are busy. It's no use complaining that you are in the middle of some crisis: their work involves crises too!

Gaining credibility with other professionals

Credibility is earned, not given on demand. Establishing a track record takes hard work. You build one by adhering to professional standards, by establishing a project of excellence and by keeping going. So many voluntary sector projects collapse. As I've said, it will help gain credibility if you are satisfying a felt need of other professionals – something that they long to see but cannot resource. They carry a huge burden of caring for the community and will be grateful to those who help them shoulder part of it effectively. They will want to understand your agenda, though, and initially may be wary. We don't hide the fact that we have our own agenda as Christians, but equally we need to respect the agenda of other professionals. If they refer someone to us to meet a particular need – housing, for example – our first duty is to meet that need.

Publicity and making the service known

We need to make the service known to various groups of people including:

- The client group.
- Other organisations and professionals.
- Other churches.
- Potential staff and helpers.

Publicity can be a mixed blessing. In order to decide whether it may be helpful or detrimental to our objectives at any one time, I ask myself a series of questions:

- What is my goal in advertising?
- At whom are we aiming this publicity? Will it reach them and be understood?
- Is it of excellent quality, true and up to date?
- Might it attract the wrong kind of attention? Becoming the next attraction on the Christian circuit can be particularly unhelpful if it happens while the project is still being established.
- Do we have the expertise to offer the services we are

advertising? Glorifying God is one thing; overstating claims is another. Are we being honest or offering quick fixes when we know things take time?

Publicity options include:

- Personal contact.
- Printed material – letters, posters, brochures, tracts, magazines.
- Speaking engagements.
- Stands at conferences and exhibitions.
- Press releases, advertising, TV and radio.

Some of these will remain more within your control than others.

7

Building on Good Foundations

The Hostel

Once I had established things properly at the Clarendon Street Discipleship House, I began thinking and praying about the Hostel. Someone in our church worked for the local council's housing department, identifying needs and finding properties to satisfy them. Though he had no idea what we were looking for, he said to me one day, 'I've found a ten-bedroom house which is too small to be of use to us right now. I wonder if it would be any good for you?' Bright and modern, it had been purpose-built as an old people's home, with good-sized communal rooms and kitchens. It would be perfect!

I drew up a proposal and went to see the people leasing the property. 'What chance do you think we've got?' I asked.

'There's really no chance we'd give it to you,' they said, looking at me as though I was far too young to take on such a project. Had I been working in the professional field, they might have taken a different view!

'OK,' I persisted, 'in percentage terms, how do you rate our chances?'

'Ten per cent.'

'OK. We'll pray!' I said.

In the end one other charity, besides ourselves, remained interested in the property. Up to then all parties' solicitors had examined the conditions of the lease, but then they read the small print of the freehold which stipulated that it had to be used by a charity operating in North Bedfordshire. The headquarters of the other organisation lay in South Bedfordshire, which disqualified them, and that left only us.

We signed the agreement. The only snag was that, while housing benefit would pay the rent, it would take about six months to come through. We needed £12,000 up front to start the venture, but we had no money.

'How are you financing this?' David wanted to know, a few weeks before we were due to open the Hostel.

'Don't ask!' I said. When I started the first house, I'd tried the health authorities in the November.

'Ring back in May,' they said. When I wondered why May, they explained, 'Because you'll have crashed by then and won't need the money!' When I enquired about our becoming a registered care home they appeared sceptical. One of them even said, 'Fancy yourself as the next Mother Teresa, do you?'

Today we enjoy a good working relationship with the secular authorities but at the beginning, when we needed their support, they doubted our competence. We had to rely on God. From Hong Kong I'd seen that he could make it possible to start something big without throwing lots of money at it. It costs, of course. It costs everything in terms of laying down our possessions and our lives in obedience to God. *Then* he provides, and yet ...

money kept arriving out of the blue to finance Jackie's work in Hong Kong. But half the Christian world knew about that. We'd only just begun in Bedford. No one had heard of us. Why should they send us money? For various reasons we only ever talked publicly about the project's financial need once to our own church and since then I've never felt particular freedom to talk about these things.

I didn't waste very much time doubting but clung to my belief that if God asks you to do something and you obey by going ahead, he *will* provide the means, even if he tests you by supplying them at the very last minute. I kept praying. Two weeks before the Hostel was to open, a couple from church phoned the office and invited David and me to lunch.

'We've a proposition to make,' was the opening gambit. 'We want to give £12,000 to your ministry. Would it be of any use to you?'

Not only did that money serve as our cash flow for some time, but our friends' timely gift confirmed to us that God was behind the project, authenticating what we were doing.

I had asked staff member Jackie Campbell to lead the Hostel and worked closely with her in its planning. Determined to establish standards of excellence right from the beginning, I found everything worked much easier this time, because I had thought out most of the ground rules prior to opening. One thing I've learnt (and which I pass on to others who are thinking of setting up projects) is that you will establish far less than you hope for in the first year. If you keep going though, you gain experience and will establish more in the first five years

than you would have believed possible. I often advise
people who are planning a project to halve the amount
they expect to achieve in the first year, but to be much
more optimistic about their predictions of growth over
five years.

Hoping the Hostel would open at the end of 1991, in
faith I doubled our staff. All worked together at
Clarendon Street, undergoing an intense period of training. In the event, various delays meant the Hostel didn't
open until April 1992. A week beforehand, Jackie fell ill
and needed an operation which kept her out of action
for several months. I worked hard to bring two other
staff members, Pete and Troy, up to speed. Despite this
last-minute hitch, the staff were so well trained and prepared that the Hostel worked like a dream from day one
and has never looked back. We took in four residents the
first week, followed by another four in the second, and
so on, until all twelve beds were filled.

We have three bedrooms for the staff, who continue to
live in at the Hostel. Although residents don't have to be
Christians, again we are up front about Jesus. On
Monday nights at the moment we have what we call CY
meetings (e.g. see why – CY – Pete became a Christian)
with stories and testimony. Usually staff will pray for
residents who are free to wander in and out of the meetings – and they do! We soon know when they become
bored!

The Night Shelter – and the Hotel

I'd sat on a committee called 'The Substance Misuse
Accommodation Group' which talked for years about

the need to open a night shelter in Bedford, but it never happened. Someone had to take the plunge!

Although my team had got to know many who slept rough, even we weren't sure how willing they might be to stay in a night shelter, since ours would be the first in Bedford. Yet we knew that our income would depend on their housing benefit and that empty rooms would spell disaster financially. Nicki, in particular, worked hard building relationships on the streets, so that people would feel comfortable coming up to the Shelter.

We had the building already in Clarendon Street, but we were using it as the original Discipleship House. Numbers there had grown and we needed more space – we had been looking everywhere for larger premises. I believe that if you work to do everything in your power, God often steps in and surprises you with exactly what is needed. I pushed at every door and followed every channel I could think of. And then I remembered a contact in one of the Bedfordshire housing associations. He explained that they couldn't finance us because of a conflict of interest between their equal opportunities policy and our Christian foundation. 'But,' he said, 'I wonder if you might be interested in this?' He handed me a brochure for the Clarendon House Hotel. 'It landed on my desk the other day and we have no use for it.'

We went to look at the place, a rambling fifteen-bedroomed hotel, then negotiated a rent of £2,400 a month. Though in a different part of Bedford, even its name fitted amazingly well, since by then we were calling our work the 'Clarendon Street Project'.

I realised that if we went ahead with this it would be

a huge task. We would be moving the project from one house to another at the same time as taking on a new ministry. I had to think through all the logistics. With most of our income coming from housing benefit, we couldn't afford to rent an unoccupied property. I thought it might be tricky converting the old Discipleship House into a night shelter within the three-day time window which was all we allowed ourselves. But we planned everything down to the last detail and it went without a hitch. On the opening two nights three residents booked into the Shelter – exactly the number we needed to break even. On the third night six came, and now all eighteen beds are full most nights.

One guy who arrived from prison recently said, 'I've dreamt of living in a place like this, but never thought I would do!' We hear horrific tales of dormitory-style hostels where residents are too frightened to sleep, but Clarendon Street has gained such a good reputation among the homeless that many travel miles to spend the night there. A handful have made it their semi-permanent home. In fact, such was the demand that David, myself and other couples from the church regularly took in the overflow from the Night Shelter.

Once up and running in May 1993, we found real support from the town as well as from the churches. Local schools have made the Shelter their special charity. Companies drop off goods which are surplus to requirements, from furniture to hundreds of tiny bottles of shampoo. We've been given enough cheese to last for months in our freezers, a tea shop donates its leftover food each day and at Christmas the place has been full of offerings from the classiest food stores in town.

Residents dined on salmon and caviar one year! It felt like the banquet in Luke 14:13!

Residents arrive for a variety of reasons. They may be referred by the police or social services, or occasionally by the Samaritans or Salvation Army. Most hear of it by word of mouth. Some have been thrown out of their homes by parents or partners or because of threats from neighbours; others have mental health difficulties. Bedford has a women's refuge which helps to explain why men make up the vast majority of those who use our Night Shelter. We have four four-bedded rooms and one two-bedded, which means we can be flexible as to ratios between the genders.

At present an average of sixty-five different residents come through the Night Shelter in any one month. At any one time two or three may be living there for over a year, but others stay for one or two nights only. If people are not ready to move on, unlike some short-stay night shelters, we do not make them leave. Those booked in to return the next night may store a limited number of personal possessions at the Hostel between the hours of 9am and 7pm, when the Shelter is closed.

When people arrive at 7pm, we give them a hot meal and afterwards they may use one of two lounges. We have televisions in both, but, as some find loud conversation intimidating, we have established a room where people can choose to be quieter.

Though we never ram Christianity down people's throats, it's clear from the minute they walk in that this is a Christian-run shelter. Incredibly few are put off. Most ask questions while filling in their forms like, 'The King's Arms is a funny name for a church, isn't it?' or

'Why's no one told me about Jesus before?' Many even find themselves asking for prayer. If we see someone in pain, we explain that Jesus healed people and ask if he would like us to pray in Jesus' name. The residents themselves asked us to run a house group for them on Monday nights, so that they could worship.

Many staff are available in the evenings. Later on, often between ten and midnight, when things have become a little quieter, people have amazing conversations about Jesus. Some go on from here to the Discipleship House – at the time of writing two of its residents have come via the Night Shelter and Hostel. Most others are Christians who for one reason or another need intensive discipleship.

Halfway houses

Having wanted to establish the final stage of the project for a long time, I had developed all the underlying thinking, the rules and regulations. But I had no leader to take it on. Though this was a small-scale project, the time didn't seem to be right.

Then in 1995, while I lay in hospital, having just given birth to twins, God said, 'Now's the time!' Put like that it sounds ridiculous, but in fact it took me a total of four hours to recruit the leaders and to firm up the guidelines and procedures. It proved easy to find a small house to rent and the fourth stage went live.

Each fourth stage house runs for nine months or so and then either the handful of residents move out or the leader does, and we start again with a new group somewhere else. It acts as a bridge to independent living,

though many don't need this final confidence-building
training in life skills. Before we established the halfway
houses, people moved into secular employment or, if
they wanted to, returned to the project as staff. We
ensured they worked in a house different from the one
they had just left, e.g. if they had been living in the
Discipleship House they had to work in the Night
Shelter or Hostel, at least for a while.

Today our second halfway house is led by Gail, whose
story is told in Chapter 9. We met her when she became
one of our first 'proper' residents in Clarendon Street.
Since then she has come through her difficulties, and,
with her husband and two children, provides a brilliant
role model.

Finance

I've written a good deal about money in this chapter –
where it came from, how God worked miracles – but also
how we used 'normal' sources of funding such as
housing benefit. God activates 'normal' channels too
and obtaining grants can be just as much a miracle as
some anonymous donation.

Sometimes I'm tempted to add up all sources of likely
grants or donations instead of trusting God whose
wealth is infinite. I have to remember that when God
called us, we had nothing. Almost all of us involved on
the project have been young people, without careers
behind us or large sums tucked away in savings accounts,
yet we're running four houses with a turnover of more
than £200,000 a year. In the end, outside funding or not,
I have to put my faith in God as Provider.

God could choose someone who had enough money to start a project, but no one's personal funds would last for ever. It would be all too easy to become isolated and fall into debt. A project stands a better chance of running long-term if the financial issue is tackled on two levels: by praying constantly and by seeking funding.

I used to read through those great chapters, Hebrews 11 and 12, and claim their promises for myself and the project. 'Even though she didn't have a clue what she was doing, even though her staff were all totally untrained and the project full of weaknesses, yet she was able to develop an effective ministry to the poor because she considered him faithful who had made the promise. And therefore from this one person, and she as good as dead most of the time(!), came descendants as numerous as the stars in the sky and as countless as the sand on the seashore!'

I don't believe that you can ever win the battle of faith once and for all. Every new financial need provides a fresh challenge. I've recorded how, quite miraculously, £12,000 came in for the Hostel, and we've received even larger sums on other occasions. Nevertheless, if we need thousands tomorrow, I'll still have to make the choice then to live by faith. In that sense it's never a done deal and it doesn't get any easier!

For those thinking of setting up a project, I've drawn up lists of some of the things which need to be considered around the whole area of finance. For matters applicable to the UK only, see Appendix 6.

A mindset of faith

Put your faith in God but, as leader, take full responsibility to make sure the finance is covered and managed properly. Faith is not an excuse for abdication. If you do not know where the money is coming from, 'by faith' is not the answer, unless you have wrestled with God and come to a firm place of faith.

Tithing

Tithing all gifts to the ministry is a powerful thing to do because it means you are trusting the financial health of the project to God. However, when large sums, such as housing benefit, come from taxpayers' money, they are intended for specific purposes. You have to ask the question: Is it appropriate to tithe this money, or indeed to give any part of it away?

Setting a budget

Sit down at the start of the year and work out likely costs for everything you can think of. For our project that would include running costs like rent, council tax, gas, electricity, telephone, post, food, toiletries, detergents, first aid supplies, staffing, accountancy fees. We would add in planned capital costs like purchasing a new car or kitchen equipment, then increase the budget by 10 per cent to cover emergencies.

Contingency fund

On our turnover of £200,000, a 10 per cent contingency fund of £20,000 sounds a lot, but it soon goes! I made a list, one year, of unbudgeted 'extras'. Some we could not have predicted. Our car locks were destroyed and a number of windows broken in the houses. A staff member had a parking fine, new fire regulations came into force and a fire gutted the front room of the Night

Shelter. All our second-hand fridges and freezers, plus some washing machines, a tumble drier and some beds and plumbing needed replacing in that one year. Our insurers requested that we buy a safe for each of the houses. Other things we should have foreseen. That year we forgot to budget for Christmas and for our trip to Stoneleigh Bible Week, both of which proved expensive.

Sources of funding

(a) Capital funding If you need a building and buy it, rather than renting as we have done, obviously you will incur greater capital but fewer operational costs. Most projects will incur some capital costs, though. Ours have included things like putting in fire escapes, showers and industrial-strength washing machines. Government, housing association, charitable trust and private sector grants are usually given only to fund-named capital costs. They may also prevent you expressing the type of ministry to which God has called you, by limiting your choice of staff or residents, for example.

I will list some of the UK sources of these grants in Appendix 6, but would warn at this point that pursuing such funding can sap all your time and energy and, with many other charities bidding for the same pool of money, you have no guarantee of receiving a penny. Don't let yourself as leader become too absorbed by this side of things. If you decide to pursue it, delegate! I have found the best source is through personal contacts of people involved in the project – because people prefer to give to projects where they know someone, rather than to some huge anonymous charity.

(b) Operational funding I would say, in most countries, go and talk to your local authority. Find out what their obligations are by law. If they have to provide housing or social care and you do it for them, then they are more likely to make available money (or even, as happened in Hong Kong, buildings).

Make friends with your social services, health, education and housing departments, as applicable. Ask them about their priorities and what they would most like to do if they had enough money. My vision in Bedford was very specific. Obviously don't compromise your God-given vision, but if you have a desire merely to *do something* for the poor, then ask the authorities about the extent of the real needs. They may fall over themselves to help you if your project covers their priorities.

If you are a charity, you should also look into the whole question of tax relief.

Accountability

Think of the number of scandals to do with financial fraud in the church this century. None of us is immune! Undertaking a large project means handling huge amounts of money and, if temptation is not to turn to sin somewhere along the line, you need to build in some careful checks and balances.

(a) Make yourselves accountable to a group of impartial individuals, such as a council of reference or the eldership of your church.
(b) Hold financial meetings monthly. It's all too easy to let 'boring' financial matters slip and so lose track of large sums of money.

(c) Open your accounts to all, at any time, and encourage questions.

(d) Don't have any one person responsible for transactions. Cheques should be signed by two people, neither of whom runs the petty cash. Never pre-sign them. Don't let the same person be treasurer or run the petty cash for years at a time.

(e) Arrange for your accounts to be audited or examined by an accountant to fulfil all legal requirements. (Don't forget to budget for this!) In addition, keep your accounts under headings which will help you see how much you are spending at any one time, will highlight overspending in a particular area and will help you keep to budget as the year progresses.

8

Onto the Streets

A church in the centre of Bedford

If my vision was to work among the poor, David's was
to plant a church where, among other things, the poor
would be welcome. He had almost forgotten God's
promise that if he would be faithful and lead the
Frontier Teams, then God would grant his vision of
planting a church that would include the poor in the
centre of Bedford. As his vision started stirring again, so
God confirmed his word in many powerful ways.

In January 1992, with the support of the leadership
of Woodside, David talked to the thirty or so people in
our house group. Explaining his vision, he asked if
any of them wanted to come with us, with the ultimate
aim of planting a church in the town centre. Nearly
everyone did. Numbers grew, so I started leading a
second house group. Then David and I led two each
and finally Jackie Campbell led a fifth. In six months
ninety people became involved. David and I left the
house groups to start a new group for leaders, plus
public meetings once a month. By the October, when we
began holding weekly public meetings in the centre of

Bedford, around 120 came along. Their average age was twenty-four.

We weren't wanting to start a youth church. Indeed, God had said to David, 'I will draw to you rich and poor, old and young.' We were happy to embrace all of those. Realising that any church culture will attract some and repel others, we chose the style of music and preaching to look and feel like us; you could say we packaged eternal truths for a new generation. For example we found that single young people didn't want to get out of bed on a Sunday morning. (David jokes this is the one time of his life when he's enjoyed the luxury of reading the Sunday papers in bed.) So we met to worship on Sunday evenings and we held lots of parties. We used to say to new people who joined us, 'Do you have any friends who don't go to church but who will come to this party, if we promise not to mention Jesus?' When they turned up their main questions were 'Do these people like me and are they fun?' So long as they felt at home and enjoyed themselves, many ended up getting involved in the church.

We had some amazing prayer meetings where God was on the move. They were so packed that you could hardly breathe and we thought the floorboards would break beneath our feet. We saw God moving in incredibly exciting ways on the project. There was always something real to pray about and miraculous answers to prayer. Intercessors began to emerge, as well as people who heard from God prophetically.

Young, on fire, radical types came to join us. Some were already Christians and had arrived in Bedford as students. About half became Christians through us, and not only through the project or Friday night meeting. Six girls became Christians in the sixth form of one of the local schools. One of them, Clare, has been co-leading the project until recently. In fact, many of those who now lead the church found Jesus at that time, but for the first four years we were helping them sort themselves out and develop leadership gifts.

By June 1993, eighteen months after starting, we found ourselves with 200 mainly immature, broken young people who nevertheless wanted to go on with God. To express its contemporary and friendly nature we named the new congregation the King's Arms. It's open to all – like a pub – and the King holds his arms open to all. By 1994 it had become a proper plant – a church in its own right, under the NFI umbrella.

A further way the church grew was through the recruitment of staff to the project. They started coming from all over Britain and latterly others have come from many countries to learn, to train and eventually to go back and start something at home. But in the meanwhile they have contributed much to the King's Arms.

The poor on the streets

I had seen from Hong Kong that it's unwise to work alone, putting all your eggs in one basket. You need both a team of workers and a pool of people from which to draw. Out of sixty you may find one or two who are genuinely ready to respond to God and undergo discipleship in a residential setting. Meanwhile you go on developing relationships with those not on the programme, building up trust and credibility. Then if one of your residents runs away, as they will, you won't feel so devastated. Even if that resident does not return, there will be others.

It's really important, before setting up a project, that you prove your ability to work in that area or with that particular people group. Unless you have contacts already and get on well with them, there's no point even starting. I knew how vital it was to keep going out to meet needy people, and I loved doing so. While I find polite society a little, well, uneventful, the unpredictability of being with needy people is exhilarating, and many are so open to spiritual things. Often the first time they hear about Jesus is from us and, because they have no trouble recognising their great need, often they are willing to 'give God a go' almost straightaway. Though sometimes they act aggressively, the Bible is right when it says, 'A gentle answer turns away wrath' (Proverbs 15:1).

We found the traditional singing/drama/preaching on street corners didn't work too well. Our contacts came mainly through those we'd made already as they brought their friends along, but I would meet more as I walked round town every Thursday afternoon, stopping for a chat in the places where street people hung about – Pigeon Square, in various alleyways or in the coffee area in the library. As people grew to know and trust me, I'd invite them back to Friday night meetings.

This kind of outreach continues even now. Simon Allen has always been particularly involved. He leads the project now, but when Simon arrived for a college course in Bedford, he was a keen young Aston Villa fan and a backslidden Christian. Even before he set eyes on the town, though, God spoke to him. 'You'll find a church where people are working with the poor, and that's what I want you to do.'

He found our church almost straightaway, got right with God and spent all his spare time as a volunteer at the Night Shelter. Then God told him to go to the dark places in the town, looking for the poor. 'Sit with them there, just be with them. Don't clean your teeth or wash for a couple of days, so you know what it is like to live in a dishevelled state. Fast for these people, give away your clothing.'

Simon found one guy who had been living rough in a railway shed for four years. At first he said very little, but seemed to enjoy Simon telling him stories about Jesus. One day, he uttered his first sentence, 'Do you really think Jesus can heal me?' Amazed at this sudden show of vulnerability, Simon prayed for him.

He met another man who had worked as a train driver, but had become a recluse after someone committed suicide by jumping in front of his train. Simon developed a special soft spot for him when he found they shared a birthday. Later he discovered that the man wasn't elderly, as he'd thought, but in his early forties. He wasn't welcome in town.

'I can't go in there!' he'd say when Simon tried to take him to a shop or café.

'Why not?'

'I'm not allowed. The man will shout at me!'

He came to live on the project for two or three years. Much of his sense of rejection disappeared and he did change, though he's living rough again now.

It takes time to build relationships of any kind, let

alone with those living on the edge. Recently Simon wrote about this in the project's newsletter:

'Think of the person who is sitting in a shop front begging or the old crippled woman who is living at home alone. How will Jesus reach their lives and bring miraculous change? Maybe his plan is to use you!

'The biggest challenge is TIME. Spend time with people. There are appointments with the power of God waiting to be unlocked by a simple pause in your daily routine. Hidden in the ordinary are the opportunities to see the miraculous. Be open and prepared for this to happen.'

God spoke very specifically to Simon about the really dark places through the Bible verse, 'Where the Spirit of the Lord is, there is freedom' (2 Corinthians 3:17).

'You have my Spirit within you. If you go to the darkest, dirtiest, most dangerous places, you will bring my Spirit there. You will bring the possibility of my freedom to those who have become stuck there.'

Most often Simon went alone, not wanting to presume that God had given the same instruction or promise to anyone else. It took a special courage to keep returning to these hidden, filthy, dangerous places, night after night. The worst, he reckoned, was a huge abandoned plastics factory, which has been pulled down now. He had to climb over corrugated iron and a wall to get in and then discovered a maze of vandalised corridors, their walls covered with graffiti spelling out which gang held sway over each part. Never knowing what he would find around the next corner, he prayed hard in tongues the whole time.

One night he stumbled across a man sleeping in one of

the rooms. He had swept the floor and arranged his spent matches in a pattern, as though to make that dangerous place his home. Simon invited him back to our Hostel and he lived there for four years. These days he finds it too busy and noisy, so he sleeps in a shed – but still turns up most mornings for breakfast.

Both our staff and church volunteers who work on the streets get used to handling difficult and violent people. Again Simon, travelling back to Bedford late at night, found the train terrorised by a man rushing up and down between carriages, hurling rubbish about and shouting. Simon managed to calm him. 'Are you OK?' he asked. 'Do you have anywhere to sleep tonight?'

'You're not going to convert me!' the man said, though Simon had not mentioned Jesus. Later Simon took the man, a schizophrenic, back to the Night Shelter. He stayed for three nights but had to leave because his shouting fits disturbed others who were trying to sleep.

Friday night meetings

These began in Clarendon Street's kitchen in October 1989, but soon split in two – one for the sober and a slightly slowed-down version in an adjoining room for the drunk. You were never quite sure what words were being sung in the latter! Forty-five or so would drift up from the soup kitchen in Bedford's town centre and perch around the sink, on the work surfaces, anywhere.

People would bring their fights into the house, or their anger against some official who had offended them. With so many potentially violent individuals squashed in small spaces and emotions running high, anything could have happened, but I have to confess that I was happiest in a potentially volatile environment. These needy people were so responsive. New staff and volunteers, as well as residents and guys from the streets, all wanted to come along on Friday nights because the Holy Spirit was moving. This was far more exciting than anything in the best of church services! Once people experienced Friday nights they wanted to stay on the project.

After a time of worship I'd start a question and answer session or a debate on matters relevant to the lives of these damaged individuals. As we looked at the story of the woman caught in adultery in John's Gospel, or discussed what the Bible said about choosing life or death, I'd home in on really practical issues, asking lots of questions. 'How would you feel if Jesus was here now, sitting beside you?' 'If Jesus knew what you'd done wrong today and told you to go and sin no more, what would you say?' 'Who here is mourning? Who is brokenhearted?' Most would indicate that they were. I'd hear their stories – a woman's child had been taken from her and put in care; a man had lost his girl, his home and all his possessions during a spell in prison. We would talk about these things and how God felt about them too.

Then they would ask us to pray for them. God can do amazing things when people come to him knowing they have great need. Those ministry times proved so powerful that when new people arrived we learnt to keep the prayer groups small, or they tended to become volatile. We must have been meeting real needs though, as week by week they brought more friends along until we had to move the meetings to a larger venue in town.

At Clarendon Street I used to perch on a high stool by

the big kitchen table and one old man known as Badger always used to sit close by my side, heckling. I'd met him in Pigeon Square. He was one of an Irish family of twelve and as cynical as they come. The others told us, 'You'll never get Badger.' But he did become a Christian, and after some guys beat him up one day he came to live on the project. We loved him for his wicked sense of humour and for the way he softened and changed. After a number of years with us he ended his days in a home which offered proper nursing care, and he died trusting in Jesus.

9

Chaotic Lifestyles

I first met Gina at one of our outreach meetings in the town centre. On being introduced she recoiled from me and dropped her gaze. It took a while before this twenty-three-year-old could utter a word. As I got to know her over the following years, sometimes she behaved with a childlike submissiveness and at others would indulge in great outbursts of anger and violence, smashing anything within range. Desperate for love, with a child in care, numerous miscarriages and at least one abortion, she abused her body through drugs, alcohol and sexual promiscuity. Her marriage, to a highly unstable man who knocked her around, lasted a weekend.

Why? Don't you sometimes wonder what goes on in the thinking of someone like Gina? What experiences have formed a mindset like that? What sets up the destructive patterns of behaviour and relationships? Can they be broken?

The problems of some individuals seem so great, their lifestyles so chaotic, that many Christians give up. They no longer believe in freedom for these people. When someone has such a chaotic lifestyle it's not always obvious where to start. How do you communicate, show them love and meet their underlying needs? Can such a person really find deliverance and salvation? I believe with all my heart that they can, but those who try to help them must count the cost. No one ever said it would be easy.

Chaotic lifestyles affect others

If a number of people with chaotic lifestyles live in the same house all kinds of trouble will result, from the serious to the light-hearted. At the Night Shelter it happened that staff member Pete was sharing his room with Badger, the elderly Irishman who had become a Christian. In the small hours Pete awoke to hear the sound of running water.

'Are you going to the toilet, Badger?' he asked. Badger suffered from arthritis and, when he lived in his own place, kept a bucket by the side of his bed.

'No!' came the reply, but in the morning Pete discovered one of the drawers all wet inside. He wasn't so keen to share his room after that!

On a good day most of us can handle trivial incidents, but when the chaos caused by our residents started affecting the lives of our neighbours, we had to do something about it. Even now, though we have all kinds of boundaries in place, incidents still happen but we've found that talking to the neighbours and inviting them round dispels their worst fear: their fear of the unknown.

When our new neighbours tried to shut us down, perhaps the real breakthrough came after one of the residents left a blanket drying on top of an electric heater, setting the front room of the Night Shelter on fire. Our hearts sank. Here was all the proof they needed that the Night Shelter was running out of control. Yet our neighbour, seeing the staff waiting in the road while the fire service drenched the place with water, invited them in and gave them tea and cakes. It turned out that she and her husband had incredibly kind hearts, and once they had got to know us as people, once they understood what we were doing, and had found reassurance about safety considerations, they did all they could to help us.

These days we would always go to talk to people in the road after any incident which affected them, and the house leader visits them at least twice a year anyway. We invite them to look round the Shelter. We give them our phone number, tell them they are welcome to call any time of day or night and we promise to take action if anything about our work worries them.

That's important because our residents *will* cause problems. Over the years I have sat through countless staff meetings discussing whom we should take in. All too often I've heard comments like, 'We can't work with him because he has a gambling problem, or abuses children, or doesn't want to work, or lies compulsively and has a rebellious attitude.' It is precisely because of these issues that we are called to stand by these individuals. There is no such thing as the perfect person to minister to. Sometimes I wonder if I myself would have the courage to change my life as much as we've asked people like Gina or Badger to change theirs.

How does God see the problems?

I have to go back to the way God sees us. We are all made in his image (Genesis 1:27). Each person is immensely valuable to him, whether it's you, me, the Archbishop or Gina. As believers we were all 'bought with a price' (1 Corinthians 6:20). But how do individuals know they are that valuable to Jesus? They may never do so unless we communicate that they are valuable to us too; unless we show them care and spend time listening to what is important to them, allowing them to be part of our lives.

But at the same time we have to remember that God sees each of us as responsible for our own sin. People often blame parents or events for the way they are but God calls us responsible. 'In those days people will no longer say, "The fathers have eaten sour grapes, and the children's teeth are set on edge." Instead, everyone will die for his own sin; whoever eats sour grapes – his own teeth will be set on edge' (Jeremiah 31:29–30).

It is clear that we can no longer say, 'I am a victim and that is why I am as I am. Poor me!' I cannot say, 'Well, because my father did this or that, then I have to be like this.' No, I have to accept that I am held responsible for my own sin and for my own response to whatever has happened.

New helpers at the Night Shelter often make the mistake of exclaiming that the old men who stay there are 'sweet', 'lovely' and 'gorgeous'. They're wrong. Of course each *is* immensely precious, but their lives are a mess and they often cause all kinds of damage to other people. So many say, 'You're making me do this,' or 'I'm like this because of my family!' But true healing can start only when they themselves take responsibility.

If you are to walk someone out of a chaotic lifestyle and if you are to see Isaiah 61 come to pass – the oppressed set free, the broken-hearted comforted, the poor receiving good news – then you need a correct biblical understanding of God's grace, truth and hope.

In the early days I would be amazed at some of our helpers if I asked them to persevere with someone who was kicking mud in their face. They would be thrown totally because they were still struggling with basic Christian principles like forgiveness. Some would lose hope when a resident let them down, maybe for the fifteenth time. Others wouldn't draw the line with someone who was out of order, or couldn't see that an individual who had been hurt by life was nevertheless still responsible for his sin.

It's a fact of life that some of the people you are trying to help will run away. I'm often asked the question, 'Aren't you in danger of being taken for a ride?' The answer is, yes of course we are. But I'm always reminded of the story Jesus told about the weeds growing among the wheat (Matthew 13:24–30.) If we uproot what we think are weeds, we'll uproot the wheat too. Come harvest time, God alone will judge. Until then he gives us personal responsibility to choose ways which lead to life ... or death.

It's a fact of life too that some people will respond to all our sacrificial love and care with abuse. They'll show no gratitude. But people in the Bible acted in those ways towards God, and so do we at times. He doesn't get discouraged. He neither lets us get away with it nor gives up on us, and that's how we're to be.

I've deliberately told many stories in this book which

have a negative outcome, because that is what can happen. I'm not intending to spread gloom but to encourage others. If someone you're trying to help takes a huge step backwards it's not necessarily your fault. Instead of assuming you've failed you need to realise such things are part of life with these people. God has given all of us free will. People can choose to turn their back on help. Equally, if they choose to accept it – and keep choosing to ally themselves with the will of God – then they will begin to change.

Gail's story

We first met Gail back in 1989 through Karen, one of David's young Frontier Team who was doing a survey in the town centre. When she asked Gail, 'What are you thinking of doing tonight?' Gail replied, dully, 'I'll probably kill myself.'

'Oh,' said Karen, wondering wildly how to help this young woman who appeared so vulnerable. 'Do you fancy a cup of coffee?' In a nearby café she learnt that Gail was taking a lunch break from her routine at the psychiatric day hospital. She tried to talk about God but Gail was sceptical.

'My dad used to preach Sundays,' she said in her Belfast accent, 'but that didn't stop him and me mum arguing all the time, or Mum walking out when I was eleven.'

There seemed little Karen could do and Gail returned to spend the rest of the day at hospital. A few months later, when Karen was visiting someone else in the hospital, she recognised Gail, who had been admitted after taking an overdose. Visiting every day, Karen learnt something of her history.

Gail had started truanting from school after her mother had walked out. She swallowed her mother's Valium and sleeping pills, along with alcohol sometimes, and by the age of fifteen had also developed anorexic tendencies. At sixteen she took an overdose, slit her wrists and ended up in a Belfast psychiatric ward, where the mental disorders of the other patients frightened her. She thought, 'If I stop eating, maybe I'll find out why I hate myself so much.' The nurses noticed, but despite their strict attention she wouldn't eat.

She found work as an auxiliary nurse but fainted on the ward one day and had to tell the doctors what was going on. Overcome by shame, she swallowed a whole bottle of sleeping pills, drank pints of cider and slit her wrists. Afterwards they told her that a couple had found her lying in a subway. By calling an ambulance they saved her life – and she spent yet more time in a psychiatric ward.

Afterwards, hoping to make a new start, Gail moved to Bedford, where her father had settled. Sharing a house with some other young people, she started drinking more heavily and taking amphetamines. The only thing she seemed to be able to control in her life was her weight, which fluctuated up and down as she alternated between eating binges and making herself sick. She was developing the binge and vomit pattern of a typical bulimic.

After her housemate's boyfriend raped her, she moved out to live on her own. Nursing on the wards she appeared to be an efficient auxiliary with a bubbly personality, but when alone in the evenings she would fall apart. Then yet another overdose landed her in the Accident and Emergency department of the hospital where she worked. She asked to be admitted to a different hospital. They pronounced that there wasn't much hope. She would have to live with her bulimia.

Later she spent ten weeks in Bedford's psychiatric Weller Wing, where a more sympathetic psychiatrist still couldn't get to the root of her problems. After leaving the hospital she frightened herself by vomiting blood, but that did not deter her from making herself sick or from taking large quantities of laxatives. That was the point at which she first met Karen.

A few months later, when Gail was back as an in-patient after another overdose, Karen asked her, 'You've tried everything else – why not try God?'

Gail didn't respond at the time but back in her own home she prayed, asking Jesus into her life – then promptly went on an eating binge and made herself sick. Feeling more guilty than ever she concluded that this Christian thing just didn't work.

Karen suggested she needed help and some stability in her life. Why didn't she move into the Discipleship House? That sounded scary to Gail. She took some convincing. She'd have to give up her dog and her independence and stop smoking. But in February 1990, three months after becoming a Christian, she moved in as one of our first residents.

We ran a Draconian regime in those days. In order to prevent her smuggling in drugs we searched Gail's belongings as she moved in and afterwards read all her post, both incoming and outgoing, lest she try to obtain any forbidden substances. She shared a small bedroom with two members of staff and for six months the only time she was alone was in the toilet – and even then someone would be knocking on the door (which had no lock) saying, 'Are you all right, Gail?' We timetabled each moment of her day, from getting up at 7am, to going to bed at 11pm. We taught her how to pray out loud in an hour's supervised quiet time each day, which included time to study the Bible together. We allowed only specifically Christian music, books and television, but Gail devoured those with a great hunger. It was fantastic to see the Bible jumping alive for her.

Quite early on she began to admit why she'd hated herself so much and we saw the real pain which all her self-destructive behaviour had sought to mask – she'd been sexually abused as a child. At that point she realised she wasn't crazy, that there was a reason for everything and a way out. She knew it wasn't going to be easy. It would take time and courage to walk it through, but by now she knew that we would support her every step of the way.

Three times a day she would have to face her great enemy in the company of laughing, joking people. At meal times guys from the Frontier Team would say all the wrong things like, 'You're looking well, Gail!' To her this meant one thing – FAT! But we prayed with her before and after every single meal. It was no longer possible for her to hide her emotions behind bingeing, pills or alcohol.

Crises continued to come and go. Gail still cut herself, which was why we had to keep such a careful eye on her. Several times she broke a glass bottle and ran the jagged edges hard up and down her bare arm. She ran off – one time she pawned her Walkman and got blind drunk on the proceeds. The first I knew was a phone call from staff member Karen, who supported herself through a part-time job at a DIY store. 'Philippa, get over here now. Gail's in the office, drunk. She's going to get me the sack!'

I bundled Gail into my car and set off for Accident and Emergency, just in case she'd taken an overdose as well as too much alcohol. A few yards down the road she threw up inside the car.

Each time, after incidents like that, she couldn't believe that we were still pleased to see her, that we would welcome her back, accepting her fully as a person, while helping her see where she had gone wrong. Each time it happened her heart softened a little more.

We had some breakthroughs, like the time I asked if she'd ever given all of herself to God – her mind, her eyes, her thighs, all the parts of herself she didn't like. She prayed out loud about each one, 'It's yours, Lord, I've given it to you.' At last she understood – her mouth was God's, she was eating for him now. She needed food to fuel her body so that it could function for him.

During one of the Friday night meetings when we prayed for her she turned numb, physically, almost as though God had given her an anaesthetic. Maybe that was exactly what she needed in order to withstand the pain of those months.

We made lots of mistakes, but on the whole, Gail did exceptionally well in the intense atmosphere of the Discipleship House. She would pray along with the rest of us if something broke and we had no money to fix it.

For example one day Jenny said, 'Lord, you know we need bunk beds. We'd really like red ones.'

The next day someone turned up on the doorstep. 'I don't know why, but I wondered if you'd like these red bunk beds?' That kind of thing happened all the time and it strengthened everyone's faith. We'd all pray, including Gail, when we hit crises with other residents too.

Meanwhile I spent hours counselling her. Afterwards she said that though we came from such different backgrounds, I seemed to understand her. She said she could understand me too because I always came straight to the point. She responded well most of the time because we trusted each other and she knew I wouldn't let her get away with things. Sometimes she tried, though, and in the July Gail experienced the worst crisis of her life.

I had been confronting her, again – this time with the fact that she was living a lie. 'Gail, you look at yourself in the mirror and you are as skinny as a rake, yet you see this fat person and feel you have to try to convince yourself that Jesus loves you anyway. You've come a long way. You *can* change. We're not playing around here.'

She went silent on me and ended up back in the psychiatric Weller Wing. Over the next few months the fact that Gail knew God only made her feel worse.

Then, in February 1991, she was ready to try again. Moving back on the same date she had moved in the first time, Gail was different now. She'd seen once again how bad life could be. By 1991 we had relaxed the regime a little and she worked part time as a nursing auxiliary, making her own choices every day not to smoke, nor to binge on the chocolates constantly available at the nurses' station.

She knew it would be hard, but knew also that she didn't have to put on a brave face or hold back her tears at the Discipleship House. She never cut herself again but she did continue to push us to the limits to see if we would still love her. Each time she proved that we did, more of her defences would melt away.

Finally she decided to qualify as a nurse, and her career was going really well until she hurt her back. By June 1992 she was ready to move out of the Discipleship House and she worked for a year in the Hotel, where other residents knew and respected her. As a counsellor she proved second to none because she knew from experience what they were going through – and the tricks they played!

She married – not easy when still working through the effects of abuse. She grew in maturity, co-leading a church house group with her husband. Later, with their two small children, they welcomed into their house a couple of girls from the project who were ready for the fourth stage programme. They made excellent progress.

It's not often that someone becomes free from eating disorders as profound as those which plagued Gail, but today her weight remains stable. She never thinks about it. She can eat anything, even chocolate, and her former destructive thought patterns have disappeared.

Walking out of a chaotic lifestyle

The gospel reverberates with this amazing dynamic of hope, because we have a powerful, forgiving God. That's a real gift to leave with someone. They don't have to settle for the way life has always been, because freedom is possible. Freedom can be frightening, though. I know how hard it is in my own life to walk out of sin, or to change my mindset and embrace the truth.

Lesley has changed, no doubt about it. She prays and she's seen God work in her life. She manages to stay in the Hostel for longer and longer periods and eventually may get her chaotic life in enough order to benefit from the Discipleship House. At the moment she keeps landing herself in a lot of trouble because she still falls foul of her temper and she still tells lies – like recounting the details of her day at college when in reality she's been nowhere near the place!

We met Caroline at the Night Shelter. She became a Christian and progressed on to the Discipleship House. Recently we've agreed it is appropriate for her to return to the Night Shelter again. There's nothing wrong with her relationship with the Lord. She prays, but she has never known structure in her life. Getting her to go to bed at 11pm is well-nigh impossible. She has no comprehension of what bedtime means, nor about doing her allotted chores, nor paying her rent. Learning those things will take time.

Greg became a Christian, was baptised and came to live in the Discipleship House, but sometimes when his pay cheque arrives he can't resist spending the lot on drink. It takes time to change if you're an alcoholic.

If someone's given themselves to drink or pornography or anger or lies for years, it's normally not God's way to wave a magic stick, do away with the person's personal responsibility and reverse the effects of their lifestyle overnight. It takes time to unlearn habits and thought patterns, and it's often a painful process. People may well dump some of the pain they feel on those who are trying to help. But, like Gail, they need to know that you will walk with them every step of the way; that even when they mess up, or run off, or hurl abuse, or go on a binge, or cut themselves, they can come back and you will welcome them with grace, mercy and consistency. So many have said, 'You knew the truth about me. You were prepared to confront me about issues, yet you loved and valued me through it all. That helped me more than anything!'

Young Richard was a classic. He caused us no end of problems. He lied about everything – there didn't have to be a reason. He took a staff member to see his mother's grave, weeping and sobbing over it. Later another staff member met his mother and commented on how well she looked for a dead person!

Richard wanted to take charge of everything, and had real problems being told what to do. When staff member Emma explained that she had to take responsibility for the cooking, he flew into a rage and started throwing things through his bedroom window – his alarm clock, his stereo, his wardrobe, even.

As the situation ran out of control the staff called in some large men from the church and also evacuated the house. That affected other residents' problems, for example an addict in mid-withdrawal from Valium had to walk around Bedford for hours in the company of a staff member. After several hours Richard grew calmer and the staff asked him to leave. The next day he came back to apologise. 'How do I control what's inside of me?' he wanted to know.

We barred him from the project for a while, then allowed him back. One day, after losing his temper with Emma, he wrecked his room and barricaded himself inside. Eventually he let a male staff member in, then regretted it. 'Get out, Pete, or I'll kill you!'

Richard had put a couple of people in wheelchairs before he arrived on the project and had ended up in a padded cell, but Pete stood his ground.

'No!' he said, quietly.

'I'll kill Emma then!'

'No.'

'I'll throw my guitar out the window.'

'No.'

'I'll play my guitar then.' He hammered out some furious punk chords, and half an hour later was playing worship songs.

Another day Richard was cleaning out a fish tank in the bathroom when it cracked. He cursed and fumed at himself. Sue, the house leader, commented gently, 'That's not the way to handle it when things go wrong.'

'How do I handle it then?' He sat down on the toilet, really upset.

Sue explained, 'It's a manageable thing. We can repair the tank – and you *can* take charge of your own anger.'

We saw Richard progress. Charming when not angry, in the church house group he would pray with perception and sensitivity, really encouraging people. Then he got into a fight with a martial arts type, the kind no one in Bedford would mess with. Richard gave him a scar, and didn't dare come back to Bedford any more. He settled in another area, joined a church, married, had a child … and went off the rails again. But he'll be back.

Spiritual help *to stop Augustine cocking up 1 corinthians to extent?*

Problems aren't just physical. You can take someone off drugs and leave them worse off if you don't help them face up to the emotional and spiritual pain which the drugs have been masking. It's not just drugs – there's rejection and abuse and plain bad choices. The decline of Christianity in this country has left a generation disorientated, with no absolutes or boundaries. They have no way of dealing with guilt or with broken relationships because they don't understand about forgiveness or repentance.

One guy was adamant. 'There's no sin in my life!' He was talking to a member of staff on night duty.

'Is that right?' she said. 'Well, I'll pray for you tonight.'

The next morning he came downstairs, head in hands, looking as though he'd not had much sleep, and admitted that he'd done some really bad things.

People need not just human help but a power greater than themselves, who understands and loves them and who will set boundaries. This is why I believe God – the Holy Spirit who draws alongside – is the only answer for so many of these people. *Yes, like in Inquisition?*

Not all who make commitments will stick with it, long-term, but some do. Damian became a Christian through our Friday night meetings at the age of eighteen. He learnt the guitar while sitting on the toilet in the Night Shelter, much to everyone's annoyance. Now they admit it was worth it because he's become one of our main worship leaders in the King's Arms! He writes many of the songs we sing and has just been on a ministry trip helping a church plant in the Lebanon.

Eight people have made Christian commitments in the Night Shelter this year. Some of those are not in a good place now but others are doing well. Jamie was always in trouble with the police and had spent time in prison. We would try to talk to him about Jesus when he stayed in the Night Shelter, but he wouldn't want to know. Something must have registered though, because when another resident declared himself an atheist, Jamie stood in the middle of the room and preached the gospel to him.

Earlier this year he became ill with violent stomach pains. When the staff offered to pray for him he said he didn't want any of 'that stuff'. In the middle of the night, as he was lying on the floor, clutching his stomach in agony, he thought perhaps he would give this praying lark a go.

'Lord, take this pain from me,' he said and the pain went instantly. After that he realised that he couldn't keep turning away from Jesus, and invited him into his life.

That wasn't the end of all his difficulties, but he did start to deal with his anger and to assume some responsibility for his own thoughts and actions. He tried to get a job, but kept being turned down on account of his criminal record. After Simon, the leader of the project, who had seen real changes in him, gave him a reference to that effect, Jamie found his first proper employment ever.

Sometimes people need more than care, prayer and counselling – they need deliverance, especially those who have been involved in occult activities. I'd never under-stood what horrific initiation rites Hell's Angels go through until I prayed for a former member who was trying to get free. What happened next was too dis-turbing to write about here, but these things are real and you do come across them. Ever since we ministered to him the former Hell's Angel has walked completely free in that area.

The first time I saw someone showing signs of demonic activity I asked Dave Devenish, 'What do I do now?' He gave me a few quick instructions and released me to get on with it. There are plenty of books on the subject, but I'd say the bottom line is to remember your spiritual authority as a child of God. He is so much more powerful than anything else!

Counselling help

Many people would be able to walk free of their prob-lems if they could see the wood for the trees. The stick-ing points have nothing to do with the effectiveness of biblical truth but come because an individual's problems are accompanied by highly charged emotions and a lack of objectivity.

Complex problems are more often than not made up of a number of simpler problems. For example the roots of eating disorders are often poor self-image, control factors, wrong family dynamics and an inability to express emotion in a correct way. Most Christians would be able to tackle any one of these without specialised counselling training. The trick is to keep one's thinking clear and to hang on for the long haul as you disentangle the entwined issues. It may take hundreds of hours. The person may want to stray all over the place, and walk out in disgust a few times, but if you keep bringing him back to the real issues, in the end he will get there.

It's wonderful when someone like Gail does gain freedom from the addictions of a chaotic lifestyle and goes on to 'comfort others with the comfort God has given her'. But the fact that many never come through doesn't invalidate God's promises. If we judge our success by chalking up apparent victories we'll be heading for disappointment. One girl lived in the Hostel for some time, became a Christian, then choked to death on her own vomit after a drinking bout. Her life had changed to some extent, but we wondered whether God knew that she hadn't the will to stick with it and was calling her home.

In the early days we made plenty of mistakes – for example we believe now that our early methods were too Draconian. While Gail feels she benefited from them, others rebelled and left the project permanently.

All anyone can do is to provide an environment where change is possible. We try to live in openness, not only telling about but showing Jesus' love, power and holiness. We listen to people, giving them time, love and care. We pray and stand in the gap for them. We confront and challenge them, we let them see the power of the Holy Spirit at work, but we can't change people. Only God can do that and he works as they take personal responsibility. Through all the ups and downs we've had to learn to measure our success not by the numbers of residents who come through, but by the extent of our obedience to Jesus.

10

Principles and Boundaries

In August 1993 I had my first baby and so took six months off from the project. Alarm bells started ringing when a staff member told me that she couldn't cope with working at the Night Shelter any longer. Inexperienced workers at any night shelter often find the volatile situations too much, but I knew this particular person was no wimp – not when she'd nursed in a busy Accident and Emergency department.

I wrote in the last chapter of how the family who had moved in next door to the Night Shelter threatened to have us closed down. We would never have planned a Night Shelter in a residential road. When we first rented it our property lay in an area full of bedsits and renowned for drug dealing, but soon afterwards developers converted two doss houses further down the road to private houses. With the economy booming, suddenly everyone was restoring the Victorian houses and families started moving in to Clarendon Street. Our new neighbour complained that activities at the Night Shelter were disrupting his family's life. His wife felt so unsafe that she dared not stay in the house with the children when he was at work. He demanded the Shelter be shut down.

On my first visit to the Night Shelter after Edward's birth I found plenty to justify both complaints. I saw an old minibus in the drive, its windows broken – apparently residents barred from the Shelter would sleep in it. The staff appeared demoralised. At eleven in the morning the breakfast dishes lay dirty all over the kitchen and no one had started on the laundry. Residents had smashed some of the furniture and doled out black eyes to one another, and the staff had suffered violence too. When on duty the house leader held things together by the sheer force of her personality, but when I talked with the other staff they seemed unclear about our principles, aims and vision.

I went back to see the neighbours. 'Give me a month to turn the Shelter round,' I said.

'There's little point. I have some experience of these things and you won't be able to,' the man replied, flatly.

I talked to my staff.

'But we have to love the residents, no matter what,' they explained, when I asked why violence and vandalism had become acceptable in the Night Shelter. They felt they had to stand there and take whatever was thrown at the project or at them. They had great hearts, were wonderful at caring for people, at laying down their lives and turning the other cheek, but we had failed to communicate to them the importance of establishing boundaries. Stuck in the midst of the situation it was hard for them to see what was happening to themselves and to others.

'Imagine you're a visitor,' I told the team, taking them

round each room in turn. 'What does it say about the people who live here if the garden's overgrown and the walls are covered in graffiti? What does it communicate if this place is rundown, and dangerous, or if we let people smash it up? What does it say about Jesus' care if we're too tired to clear up, or to hope any more that someone can conquer their anger problem? What does it say if the residents are frightened to go to sleep at night and the neighbours are terrified by running battles at all hours? We need to take a detailed look at this place and ask ourselves what kind of message we are communicating.'

I watched their faces fall even further. They must have hated me for bringing them face to face with painful reality. They had been giving of themselves way past the point where it hurt; they had taken on board all the difficult scriptures about turning the other cheek but ignored those about confronting people with their sin. I'd taught them to serve sacrificially, to go the extra mile, but, applied without wisdom or boundaries, this godly principle had led them to devalue themselves and others. What a fine line to draw – and I hadn't been around to give them support or guidance!

'Now think about how it could be and what we *could* achieve,' I said, 'because we're going to set this place to rights! You know, you don't have to live with violence or fleas. We can bar people from the premises, not just from the house. We're going to sit down together and take a good look at everything we're doing. We'll change whatever needs changing, step by step. I'll help you and we'll do this together!'

I took over the leadership of the Shelter and we

looked at everything, for example at why boundaries
were being crossed and why rules weren't enforced. To
stop trouble spilling out into the street we assigned
someone to monitor activity there – he or she would
wear a yellow jacket for clear identification. Residents
could no longer hang around the street or the garden,
causing trouble. We established carefully thought-out
rules like 'No drunks in communal areas' and 'No abuse
to staff'. After one warning, we barred people who
broke these rules. That meant they were not allowed to
come to the Night Shelter for an agreed period of time,
after which they could return pending a positive interview with the house leader, which took place away from
the premises.

We laid down procedures, such as 'Two members of
staff answer the door'. We worked out why certain jobs
were failing to get done and, whether it was putting away
the tea towels or preventing riots, we made adjustments
accordingly. We looked at safety issues including fire
regulations, medical considerations and the protection
of children.

I talked to all the neighbours, invited them round,
explained our aims and how we were changing things
and soon we had lots of new friends. Instead of trying
to shut us down the next door neighbours started donat-
ing clothes! If any untoward incidents affected the community around us, we would talk with them, listen to
their concerns and take appropriate action.

We looked at ways of improving the fabric of the
building and at upgrading the equipment we needed. We
had no money when we started, and our second-hand
electrical goods were always breaking down. We decided

we wanted to reflect Jesus' heart, not a poverty spirit, and from then on aimed for excellence rather than for something merely good. We still had no money, but staff, church and residents together prayed it in – £18,000 to revamp the hotel which now served as our Discipleship House, and plenty more for the Night Shelter. There we started a programme of redecoration. We installed central heating, new bathrooms and a kitchen. By the time we had finished the guys who came to stay said they had never seen a night shelter like it and we were able to explain, 'That's how much Jesus values you as an individual.'

To everything from laundry to diet, we applied the highest standards. We ensured everyone knew exactly what they were supposed to be doing and how to do it well. I made sure they had support where they needed it.

I realised my staff were the project's most important resource. They have always been important to me and I know that if they become demoralised through stress and overwork, the project will suffer. We looked at reasons why staff became stressed and ill, or had nightmares. I realised that we needed more staff and set about recruiting them. We started with four at the Night Shelter, now we have ten! We created new rotas and timetables. We looked at supporting staff, both as individuals and as teams. We devised better training programmes. We increased the amount of time they could take off and looked at any problems in the relationships between male and female staff members.

I have to say that the demoralised team I found that day became the best team we've ever had on the project. Most of them have gone on to lead other teams or to start new projects because, as we learnt together from mistakes of the past, we were laying strong foundations for the future.

Setting boundaries

I'd always known that we needed to set boundaries on the project, but it took us a while to work out the most appropriate level of control and supervision. On my return from Hong Kong I'd tried to implement a system I had seen work there. In our first house, staff and residents rose at seven for a compulsory supervised 'Quiet Time' of prayer and Bible study. After breakfast all would do household tasks on a rota basis and then go out to work together. (In hindsight we should have prayed in the money and used our joint labour to improve the less-than-wonderful accommodation.)

After cooking and eating their evening meal residents and staff would meet for Bible study and worship, except on house group nights – house groups and church were compulsory. Staff read incoming and outgoing post and accompanied residents at all times, in case they arranged to meet someone to obtain drugs or alcohol, or sought to harm themselves.

We spent most of our time and energy fighting unnecessary battles as we tried to enforce the rigid regime. We found these incredibly tight boundaries created conflict, mistrust and rebellion. Residents would run away in the middle of the night and staff in pyjamas would be chasing them down the road!

In Hong Kong I had worked with older addicts, semi-institutionalised from their time in prison, and they seemed to benefit from a regimented approach, but Chinese culture puts the corporate before the individual anyway. You could tell people there, 'We are all going for a walk now!' and they would go. In England, they would say, 'On your bike!'

The rigid regime meant underlying problems weren't dealt with. A simple trip to the Post Office could result in a resident bumping into someone he knew. If they had outstanding issues between them, the staff might find themselves trying to stop a fight.

Before long we realised that our methods were simply not working. We found that if we took all choice away from people they would not grow or resolve issues. Any change in their lives or spiritual development proved temporary because they failed to find the motivation for themselves.

It's true that the addicts' overriding drive to obtain drugs makes them rather like toddlers. In the early stages of rehabilitation you have to watch them all the time, but they can't live under that kind of supervision for ever. To stand any chance of remaining drug-free they must learn to make good choices for themselves.

At Clarendon Street, we were running a multi-purpose project, not a drugs rehabilitation centre like the ones in Hong Kong, and had to consider all the residents' needs. We decided to make the whole programme completely voluntary and to encourage residents to find work or places on government training and employment schemes. In August 1992, when Clarendon Street was still the Discipleship House, we discussed with residents the changes we wanted to make. We decided that we wanted it to be like a family and also to be a place where people could learn how to grow and to take on responsibility.

The changes we made – whether to the rooms, the timetable, staff responsibilities or the rules – put responsibility back on the residents. Having discussed our assumptions that they wanted to follow God, to change and to grow, we introduced goal setting and regular pastoral interviews, to help them.

In fact the voluntary programme proved chaotic – a nightmare for any kind of community living and ineffective for discipleship. Eventually we let the pendulum settle in the middle. The Discipleship House had to have more purpose than being a safe and comfortable place to live. Helping individuals set their own goals, we explained that if, after a period of time, they failed to make good choices and to work through some of their agreed objectives, then they would need to find more suitable accommodation. The Hostel was less strict but people still had to do the tasks assigned to them. In all four of our houses aggression, violence and inappropriate sexual behaviour are out of bounds.

People still kick against the structures necessary for community living. Many hate being told what to do, but some, over the years, find the discipline and respect for others which their own families failed to teach them. Recently the smile on the face of one man said it all. For years he had stayed on and off at the Night Shelter or Hostel. He'd been barred several times, but now had come to tell us that he'd held down a proper job for a whole year, and was even doing overtime so he could pay for his girlfriend's haircut.

We've learnt that the soft approach doesn't always

work. Take Heather. She came from a difficult background to live at the Discipleship House but she didn't seem that interested in sorting out her life. She was rude to staff time and time again and refused to do anything we asked. Because of this we barred her from the Discipleship House, then from the Hostel and even, finally, from the Night Shelter. Eventually she went to live at the YMCA. Because she kept sniffing glue and hanging around at the top of multi-storey car parks, in the end the police and doctors considered sectioning her under the Mental Health Act.

'They don't know what they're talking about,' she complained to Emma, who led Bedford's YMCA, and who happened to have worked on the Clarendon Street project for three years.

'Oh yes they do!' countered Emma. 'Look at the way you're living your life.'

That shocked Heather so much that she decided to do something about it. She came back to the Night Shelter, then to the Hostel and the Discipleship House – and this time she was prepared to work through her problems. In eighteen months her life had changed so much that she was ready for the Halfway House. Today she's a key member of one of our church house groups, serves on the children's work team, has been helping out as a volunteer at the Night Shelter one night a week for the past eight months and is joining the project staff in January. This is the same Heather who two-and-a-half years ago was barred from the Night Shelter. Sometimes people have to experience what it's like to try to get through on their own and then hit rock-bottom before they are willing to let others help them.

Setting boundaries and right procedures

Once you have set boundaries and rules, consistency is important. It's vital to think everything through properly at the outset – not only what the rules should be, but how you will enforce them. Right procedures will help everyone keep within the boundaries you have established. If they are set up properly, even inexperienced, immature staff members will be able to cope, because everyone will know exactly what they have to do.

Areas which you need to consider include the following:

Sanctions – methods of discipline

Many people we deal with have learnt to be controlling. They hate authority figures or being told what to do. However, for a community to work for the good of all, it is important that residents co-operate with the staff and house leader. We have established a clear set of written rules (see Appendices 1 and 2) and everyone agrees to abide by them before they take up residence. Like yellow and red cards in football, anyone who breaks these will be given a warning and, on a second serious offence, will be barred from the project (the length of time is at the staff's discretion).

Some Christians throw up their hands in horror, but discipline is scriptural. 'My son, do not despise the Lord's discipline and do not resent his rebuke, because the Lord disciplines those he loves, as a father the son he delights in' (Proverbs 3:11–12).

You need to consider whether or not you would be prepared to take out injunctions against individuals or to press charges for offences against staff and/or residents. In ten years of ministry we have never needed to do this, but decided we would if absolutely necessary. We have been pushed to the brink only twice.

Lesser offences, if repeated, are dealt with by sending the person to one of the other houses for a set period of time. For example if someone in the Hostel refuses to do chores allotted on the rota, he or she may be transferred to the Night Shelter for a couple of weeks.

We have found it best to establish a rule that if an offence involves particular members of staff, then different ones will apply the sanctions. This helps the affected staff members to feel supported and also helps prevent any errors of judgement resulting from personal involvement.

Violence

(a) What level to tolerate When working with the poor it's unrealistic to insist on no violence at all. Violence will happen if you work with people who have difficulties in controlling their anger or who are used to a violent lifestyle. One woman kicked me in the stomach about twenty times. I'd touched on a painful issue during counselling and she spun out of control.

When deciding what level of violence to tolerate every project leader will have to take into account the way violent incidents affect three groups of people:

- Obviously those you are trying to serve need to feel safe. What would be the point of going to a night shelter if you couldn't sleep for fear of being attacked? How many would queue at a soup run if word got around that people were often beaten up afterwards?

- The local community must feel safe, too, or you could be closed down. Violence in the street outside the project building will affect the neighbours and, if not dealt with, will soon spell death to any ministry. It's not only residential projects that need rules about violence – they apply to day centres, soup runs etc. In all cases it is vital to establish good relations with the local police and to lay down clear guidelines giving the circumstances in which staff should call them.

- The staff and volunteers need to feel safe, although if they are well trained in how to diffuse and deal with violent situations, if most of them are mature, confident and experienced in knowing God's protection, then they can tolerate some violence. Even so, staff will need strong support or they will suffer stress of various kinds and probably leave. Even after we improved the Night Shelter dramatically, the former Accident and Emergency nurse who had expressed her anxieties to me decided she'd had enough, and I could understand that. In fact she went to work in another of our houses.

(b) Limiting violence In the early days a serious incident would affect the project on average once a week. I would go on my own to a violent situation in the middle of the night, trusting in God to protect me. I have to say that, by his grace, he did and, despite our foolishness, no one on the project has ever been seriously injured. These days, though, we would apply more wisdom in the following areas, and violent incidents have become rare:

- We have established clear boundaries, set by the leader and upheld at all times. First of all it is important to define what you mean by violent behaviour. Does it include verbal abuse, threats and/or sexual harassment? If you accept some violence, where do you draw the line – grievous bodily harm, actual bodily harm? What about damage to or theft of property? Does it make a difference if that property belongs to the project, to staff or to other residents? What is your policy on weapons? We let no one into our hostels carrying drugs, alcohol or weapons. They are asked about these things at the door, but what happens if someone grabs a kitchen knife or breaks a milk bottle?

- We looked at the reasons why violent behaviour might occur and established rules about not annoying or endangering other occupants. We felt that certain television programmes could provoke residents to undesirable behaviour, which is why our rules ban any containing scenes of violence, sex or occultic activity. We've learnt to keep those who are drunk or high well away from other residents (see under 'Alcohol and drugs', below).

- Our staff are trained in how they should act in a potentially violent situation – to behave in the opposite spirit, remaining calm and quiet, yet to stay firm and not give ground.

- We will call on outside help where necessary. Many situations are best left to the police. We've developed a good relationship with our local station and they will come quickly when we call for help. Some mental illnesses can spark unpredictable violence and we've had to learn that these need careful handling, involving the appropriate agencies.

- We make every effort to understand individuals. Because we've spent time getting to know the people who hang around Bedford's streets, we have a good idea how each is likely to behave under the influence of alcohol or drugs. Also, they have developed a relationship of trust with us which makes violence less likely. The explosive situations tend to arise when you find yourself having to confront a stranger. If someone we don't know turns up on the doorstep of the Night Shelter, we will let them in and make it a priority to get to know them, but we have to recognise that may take time. Many find communication difficult and in the end we still find ourselves relying on God for protection.

- We've learnt certain 'rules' which govern street culture, for example it is rare for a male to attack a female, because they don't like men who hit women. It's rare for our female staff to be attacked – unless by another woman – and we find their intervention can calm a fight between men.

Given mature, experienced staff and good ground rules, most violent situations can be nipped in the bud.

(c) Dealing with the effects of violence It's important to realise that even the most mature staff left unsupported in a violent situation can end up damaged. Recently Simon, who leads the project now, was coming downstairs when he saw a Night Shelter resident backing a new member of staff against the wall and making

sexual advances to her. Simon took the man into the office, explained this behaviour was unacceptable and later barred him from the Night Shelter for a further offence. The woman, a mature Christian who had project-led her church's soup run in another town, shed tears of gratitude as well as relief. 'No one's ever offered me that kind of protection before,' she said. 'I thought we had to put up with that kind of thing – that it was part of the job.'

Today we would always discuss any serious incident with the staff involved as well as with the residents. A project leader or employer has to consider the effects of violence, especially on those staff who have a measure of brokenness themselves. If your particular staff cannot cope, then you may have to exclude some individuals even before they cause trouble.

Alcohol and drugs

Again, a clear policy needs to be established. We realised it would be unrealistic to exclude anyone under the influence of alcohol or drugs from the Night Shelter – nor would we want to. However, we don't allow drugs and alcohol on the premises and we reserve the right to refuse entry to any who appear uncontrollable. We exclude anyone we find drunk or high from communal areas. We send them to bed. This process can in itself prove challenging but, although volatile, it heads off more dangerous situations. We ban anything which could be connected with drug dealing, even talking about drugs or handing over money. This again is for the safety of all concerned.

Medical considerations

Serious infections such as HIV and hepatitis B can be spread by bodily fluids. When working with the poor they will sometimes vomit, or spill their own blood or that of others, so it is important to consider procedures. We treat everyone in our houses – staff, residents and visitors – as if they were HIV and hepatitis positive. We use gloves and bleach to clear up bodily fluids and we require all staff to be vaccinated against hepatitis B. For our sample HIV policy form, see Appendix 4.

We also observe the accepted rules of food hygiene. Standard procedures concerning cooked and uncooked meats, refrigeration, food storage and so on can appear petty but they do make sense. Some people are nervous of the environmental health department, but in fact they give sensible advice which the wise will follow.

Child protection

We find ourselves counselling many victims of abuse and it is an unfortunate fact that some who have themselves been abused go on to abuse others. Perhaps because Christians are taught always to believe the best of people, the church is not always vigilant in this area and has seen all too many scandals. That's why we try to be wise as serpents and gentle as doves.

Project leaders need to study the Children Act and take account of all its implications. For example, did you know that under-sixteens need parental permission in order to receive counselling, or to become a resident? Or that seventeen- and eighteen-year-olds can go to their careers office, claim parental estrangement and then are eligible for an equivalent of housing benefit and can live independently?

Even if a project is not working specifically with children, some may visit it – and they will certainly be part of any church. Child protection must be paramount. There are two main dangers:

1. Known abusers Christians believe that individuals can change through God's power and that we need to forgive. However, the statistics show how rare it is for someone to stop abusing children once he or she has started. People may make good progress through Christian counselling, and genuinely experience God in their lives. But, be they alcoholic, paedophile or plain, ordinary sinner, anyone may fall again. However, while the alcoholic will mess up his own life, the paedophile will devastate a child's. We would never expose known paedophiles to children, certainly not on their own. If one comes to church we assign someone to accompany them everywhere.

2. Abuse victims By no means all who have been abused go on to become abusers. Most would say they have a total abhorrence of any such thing, but again, statistics suggest that we need wisdom. It would seem foolish, even unkind, to let someone minister to children if they had not yet worked through the issues. If an abused person progresses well in counselling, makes him or herself accountable and never works alone with children, that's fine.

We would always get *anyone* working with children to

fill out a form requesting information from the police on any criminal activity in which they might have been involved.

Confidentiality

Again we have drawn up clear guidelines because this is an issue of trust. We make it clear to all staff and volunteers that they must not gossip about residents. However, our residents give permission, through the house rules which they sign, for staff to speak to anyone who is part of their problem or part of the solution. Without that agreement many problems can't be resolved. Staff exercise discretion, as it is not always appropriate to speak to all involved in the problem – or not at the time, anyway.

11

Recruiting and Keeping Staff

Rebecca came to Bedford to join a Frontier Team back in the days when I was on the staff at Woodside. I met her from time to time in the church's office and she seemed far from happy. It was bad enough for anyone to experience a crisis of faith while on an evangelistic team, yet, as a pastor's daughter, she felt she couldn't leave. As we talked, I realised she was becoming ever more disillusioned, angry and frustrated. She felt she had no control over which way her life was going.

'If you don't get this sorted out you'll self-combust!' I said to her one day, suggesting she came off the team, moved to the Discipleship House and thought about starting a college course. She almost cried with relief. Afterwards she told me that she'd needed my directness. 'You didn't say, "There, there, everything will be OK." You told me it would be tough, but somehow I saw that you weren't afraid of tough decisions if they would make things right in the long-term.'

I met with Rebecca regularly to talk things through. I could see how her anger was driving her not only to despair but to make some serious mistakes in relationships. Yet I could also see great potential in her. I asked some searching questions as to what lay at the root of her anger, which would boil up out of all proportion to any incident. Sometimes, as we talked and prayed in the specially adapted shed at the bottom of our garden, she would scream so loudly that David, back in the house, wondered what on earth the neighbours must be thinking. He would ask me to close the windows!

Often people want to change but they don't know how, so they slip into despair. I'd go step by step with Rebecca. 'If you want to change, this is what you need to do.' We'd look at her attitudes and at the ways in which she related to people and consider appropriate ways in which she could express her anger. As she lived closely with others, she saw how God was working real change in them and began to acknowledge for herself once more that this God thing was real.

In the middle of all this the Discipleship House moved to the hotel, but in spite of the busyness she continued to grow. After eight months she came on staff. It wasn't easy for the rest when she would sulk or cry her way through team meetings, have angry outbursts or refuse to worship. Some days she would be fine; others impossible. She'd become accountable to the house leader and other staff members who would not let her get away with her destructive mood swings. 'You cannot continue like this,' they said. 'Don't you see how your behaviour affects others?' She'd not thought about that too much before.

Rebecca expected that her erratic behaviour would lead to us taking responsibility away from her, but that would have been too easy a course of action for her at the time. Slowly she began to learn about responsibility.

When we first started the project, it was hardly the environment in which to encourage staff's personal growth. By the time Rebecca came on board we had gained some experience – the houses weren't as chaotic as they had been and staff did have proper time off every week – but we still had a good deal to learn. We had no shifts. Staff worked from 7.30am to 11pm. However, I would talk with Rebecca about any difficulties she experienced at work. Team members can rub each other up the wrong way, timetables can suit one person better than another, and I was prepared to consider any change which would benefit the whole team.

While at the start she was terrified to confess anything she had done wrong, slowly Rebecca learnt to trust us. She discovered that the house leader wouldn't recoil in horror but was only too willing to help her through difficult times. She and I would still meet occasionally to talk, or for prayer over counselling issues. We'd look at her relationship with the Lord, at her struggle to maintain its passion and at her long-term vision.

I spent hours with Rebecca, and I was right about her potential. Despite her struggles she proved willing to learn. She began to want to give love, rather than look for affirmation from others. She gained in confidence so much that we made her second-in-charge of the Night Shelter. In that role she learnt to look after the staff and to create a sense of team. She loved it. Someone in the church prophesied that God was reconstructing the very things which had been Rebecca's destruction and that she would use her experience for instructing others – and that is what happened. She learnt to get alongside the residents and to help them. She worked well with Simon, the Night Shelter's leader at that time – so well that in the end she married him! Today she has a responsible job as an MP's case worker. (David and I will continue to work with Rebecca and Simon because all of us are seeking to create environments where the poor can be cared for.)

Why staff join

As with everything else we made huge mistakes towards our staff, but we must have done something right. I could not have run the project without them. They worked for nothing in the early days – and had to pay their own rent! Today those in their first year live rent-free and are paid £10 a month. Obviously they are not doing this for the money, so why do they work for us, and how do we recruit them?

Rebecca's story is not untypical. Many of those who join our staff aren't totally together people, nor do they always come to us because they have a heart for the poor. Very often they see how people's lives change while working on the project, and notice how their relationship with God deepens – and they want that for themselves.

Like Rebecca, many who've arrived young and inexperienced have left the project equipped with pastoral and leadership skills, plus the confidence to hold down responsible jobs like teachers or speech therapists. One of our ex-staff has become the youngest YMCA house leader in the country. Jackie Campbell, one of our first house leaders, is ministering to the poor in Chicago and has responsibility within the church there.

I've always believed that people benefit by working on

the project. It stretches them. They find themselves in difficult situations and see first-hand that God answers prayer. Communal living, and working alongside people with major difficulties, brings to the surface any inconsistencies in their own lives and Christian walk. They can put these right in the supportive environment of the project. They learn to disciple others, to take responsibility, to be accountable, to solve problems and to take initiative. They receive special training courses. Today people from all over the world join our project because they say it's some of the best, most thorough and intense training for leadership they have ever encountered – not only for work with the poor but for church leadership too.

In the early days, I believed with a passion that coming to Bedford and working with the poor was the best thing that could possibly happen to anyone, so I would recruit staff wherever I went. David and I were invited to a whole series of friends' weddings and people would joke that I would return from each with at least one new recruit!

Role models for Christian women who wanted to lead or pioneer were thin on the ground, so some from our church joined the staff because they wanted to spend more time learning from me. For example, when I arrived to share Nicki's flat and invited Mary to stay the night or Sarah to come off drugs there, Nicki said, 'This is the kind of thing I've always wanted to do, but I didn't have the get up and go until you came along.'

To recruit staff you need a leader who will get things started and give confidence. I love taking inexperienced and broken people onto my staff, but that's part of my personal vision. It works only if the leader is prepared to give them good counselling and training, and if challenging individuals are limited to one per team.

How to recruit

I keep my recruiting antennae up wherever I go – in the supermarket, on holiday, and yes, even at weddings! It's become a lifestyle! I take every opportunity to talk publicly about our work, so as to spread the net wide, and I take a long-term view. A young, single person straight out of college may be able to move across the country and come on staff at short notice for a 'gap year'. Someone else may have other commitments in our own church, and be supporting a family through paid employment. It may take a while to arrange things so that he can join us. If I meet an old friend from another church in another geographic region and talk about our work, even if she feels God calling her to work with us, it may take longer still. It's important to keep mentioning the subject without becoming controlling or manipulative in any way.

You can advertise, but it is important to monitor the amount of time, energy and money you spend on this. If the people who respond to your advertisements differ from you in their philosophy of ministry it could cause problems. If a project is seeking to work with people on a deep spiritual level, misunderstanding could arise if staff come from differing church backgrounds.

The real answer to 'How to recruit' is prayer! 'The harvest is ready but the workers are few. Pray to the Lord of the harvest.' Miracles do happen. Many years I've thought in March, as numerous staff members decided

it was time to move on, that we would have to close
down. But by the September we would have a full
complement of staff again. When things look difficult I
have to remember that if the ministry I'm establishing
belongs to God, then he will bring people of his choice
to work with us. I believe that work with the poor should
be incredibly exciting and worthwhile. So if there's a
steady decline in staffing, I would look at whether we've
lost that dynamic in some way, and at whether we need
to make any adjustments in order to regain it. I would
pray even harder, address the issues I felt were weaknesses and expect to make some changes.

What level of staffing do you require?

This will vary considerably depending on the size and
nature of the project. A children's home for the under-
fives requires an enormous number of staff, but a
halfway house very few. Five houses require more staff
than one but there is a basic minimum for any given unit.
For example we've found that whether you have three,
seven or fourteen residents in a house, you can't make do
with fewer than five staff.

The more you undertake to do for people, the more
staff you will need. Will you care for all levels of needs –
physical, emotional and spiritual – or specialise in one
level? Will you cook, wash up and do their laundry? Who
will clean the building, do the shopping, look after the
finances and the administration? When planning a project
it's all too easy to overlook such vital roles because they
don't deal directly with the people you are serving.

What hours will your project open? If running a
lunchtime day centre you won't need to allow for differ-

ent shifts, but it's a different matter at a hostel, which never closes. When working out staffing ratios don't forget to allow time for staff to train, have team meetings and liaise with other bodies. We've found it wise to allow for one being on holiday, one sick and one on their day off at any one time. Will this leave enough staff and helpers to cover? We started with four staff effectively on duty twenty-four hours a day. The Night Shelter now has ten full-timers working three shifts by weekly rotation, with a week's recovery period after night duty. Can you make do with fewer full-time staff by using part-time volunteers? They have proved useful in the Night Shelter, especially for emergency cover, but less so at the other houses, where long-standing relationships are so important. It's wonderful to be able to call on volunteers from the church for specific tasks, for example to tackle all the practical jobs which need doing when we set up a new house. We're also really grateful to a team from the States who worked hard over a limited period of time putting in the Night Shelter's new kitchen.

The number of regular staff needed will depend on their maturity. Those who are used to working under pressure, who can take a hard knock without questioning God or asking whether they are in the right place, will be more productive and more flexible. They will be able to move from an administrative task to a counselling situation, from a potentially violent situation to a pastoral interview, without being sent reeling.

What kind of people do you need on your staff?

When starting a project from scratch, when no one knows the leader and you've not even proved yourself, you're unlikely to find a large pool of people willing to work with you. Those who do will be your greatest asset. Who they are – their characters and giftings – is what the project will become. The higher their calibre, the further you can push the ministry. High-calibre people may not become available until you have established a track record, so it's important to develop the ones you do have. If you have good systems in place, systems which almost anyone could operate, and if everyone knows what they are supposed to be doing, then you won't need incredibly high-calibre staff. Many problems and emergencies simply won't arise.

I've found it helps to ask myself various questions when deciding the kind of staff we need:

1. Would secular qualifications help? In some fields they are obligatory. For example if you want to run a nursery for underprivileged children, a certain percentage of the staff will need suitable qualifications. In other cases these aren't required by law but can prove extremely helpful, both in building credibility and with the work itself. For our project I keep my eyes open for staff with medical, counselling or social work training. To have a nurse on board, or even someone with a psychology degree, while not strictly necessary, can prove a real asset. Jackie Campbell's nursing training proved invaluable in the early days of the project. We sought her advice over medical issues and her practical help as residents cut themselves, took overdoses or faced illness. An ex-social worker on staff made us aware of social work policy and told us when we needed to inform other departments about situations.

2. What experience would be relevant? Many of our staff
are young people doing gap years and have come to gain
experience rather than to give it. Those who stay longer
than a year may gain enough on-the-job experience to be
able to take on house leadership. It's great though if
some staff bring new areas of expertise with them.
Anyone who has worked in the caring professions can
prove especially useful, but I would hesitate to make
someone, however experienced, house leader until he or
she had worked for at least a year on the project.

3. Is the ratio of male to female workers important to me?
More women than men become involved in the caring
professions. While the majority of the people we serve
on the project are men, most who apply to join our staff
are women. In the early days our lack of male staff left
me with a dilemma. I believed – still believe – that the
most effective ministry for men will come from other
men. So when needy men kept turning up on our
doorstep I wondered whether I should turn them away
because we lacked male help. Who was going to lead the
houses? The people with experience were women, but
would male staff take orders from them? I had to talk
these issues through with the leadership of my church.

4. Do I value character above gifting? The emphasis may
differ according to whether I'm looking for someone to
work with people as part of a team, or to do some specific job. A hopeless administrator could prove disastrous, however godly a person they might be! It may be
that a leader decides it is part of a project's role to take
on some with a measure of brokenness and to help them

grow as Christians. If so, they will need discipling skills and time resources at their disposal.

5. What kind of people do I need to build a good team? Totally disparate types of people aren't a good idea, nor is it good to have many broken individuals on staff.

6. Do I have a specific job description in mind? What kind of person might fulfil it?

7. How long do I expect someone to work on the project? The higher the calibre of person, the longer they will be able to cope with high pressure.

Interviews

Personally I find out more by chatting with people in the kitchen than by formal interviews with set questions. The kinds of things I ask myself and applicants are:

- Do I connect with this person?
- Could we work together? Would they respond to me? Would they be loyal?
- Would they work well in the team, being prepared to pull together and cover for others?
- What is their vision? I'd worry if it differed from ours and they appeared inflexible.
- Are they a sprinter or a plodder? I would rather work with a 'plodder' any day – sprinters may look good but they burn out!
- Am I interested in this person for their potential or for what they bring now? I've found from experience that potential can prove elusive! People perform at the level

they are at now, so if I don't think that's good enough, I shouldn't take them on board.

- Does this person appear to be Mr, Mrs or Miss Ideal? Such a person does not exist! If I think I've found one in an interview, I conclude that I haven't interviewed properly.
- Do they have two good references and a recommendation from their church? Twice I've ignored a church's warnings that a person isn't suitable. I felt that I knew better – that we could help the person – but both times I've been proved wrong.

Contracts of employment

See Appendix 3.

Keeping your staff

Why is it that someone can feel God has called them to work on a project, have a real heart for the poor, be sent by their church, yet leave disgruntled and demotivated at the end of the year? That very scenario has happened to us more than once.

Having recruited our staff, I realised that it was important for us to keep them! I've found we need to look at three main areas: working conditions, support and motivation of staff, and training. I'll deal with the last of these in Chapter 12.

Working conditions

While enjoying some success in ministry, we've lost a number of staff through stress or illness. At least two still suffer from ME as a result of working on the project, and I must take my share of responsibility for that. When Jackie Pullinger-To came to speak to Bedford churches, she gave an appeal for those who had been burnt through working with the poor to come forward. My staff were the first to rush to the front. One lay on the floor, sobbing. I too have had to learn, because I am the sort of perfectionist who will work an eighteen-hour day and only realise I'm tired when I stop. That kind of work pattern has made me ill a number of times over the years.

My staff had no choice. Their working day used to begin at 6.45am and end at 11pm. They would then be on-call all night. Because they lived in, they would most likely be disturbed at least once, only to face an early start again the next morning. They might have a couple of half-days off during the week but those new to Bedford often had nowhere to go to relax or to catch up on sleep. People are not designed to live like that – four to a tiny room, with perhaps a drawer and a half for all their belongings. We all need some space. I know I need time on my own to meditate and pray and to think things through. Jesus often drew aside to pray and to refocus. Today staff have a whole day off every week. Residents accept that and don't bother them.

We could have saved ourselves a lot of heartache by taking staff's needs into account from the beginning. I've had to learn, both in my own life and in organising the project, that all human beings need rest. Even when we introduced shifts, those on nights lived in. The day shift's work involved vacuuming the whole house, including the bedrooms where the rest were trying to sleep. Eventually we learnt and moved the Night Shelter staff off-site, apart from one who sleeps there during night shift. There's a telephone connection to the room so the two on waking duty can call him or her if necessary.

At the beginning our staff were supporting themselves and paying rent. Today housing benefit covers staff rents. We pay them a minimal amount of pocket money in their first year, because they will bring some money with them, and this first year is viewed primarily as an opportunity for service and training. We pay them more in the second and subsequent years as their initial supply of finance may well have run out.

We also learnt that to keep staff healthy and energetic we had to provide basic necessities like proper nutrition, washing facilities, heating, lighting and shelter (without leaking roofs).

We are still learning. It used to be a standing joke in the church that anyone who worked on the project became ill. When Simon and Clare took over leadership from me they recognised that this had enough truth in it to kill all our work with the poor, so they invited a local GP and a pastor to do a staff care report and took strong action on it afterwards. They wouldn't allow staff to help with street work on their days off and they made sure they used all their holiday entitlement. Christians with good hearts and missionary zeal see the need and want to spend themselves to meet it, which is only right. But leaders have a responsibility to make sure they do not damage themselves in the process. We found in particular that those new on the project would hate to stop, so leaders would have to intervene and say, 'Take a break now, or else tomorrow, when we need you, you'll be exhausted!'

Another area we had to think through was that of male/female relationships. If a couple who live in the same house start dating it can cause all sorts of problems, both for them and for the other staff and residents. We allowed no dating and no engagements on the project when we had only one house. However, we realised it wasn't healthy for the project to become too monastic. God does bring young people of similar vision together! Once we had more houses, we could move anyone who started dating, so that non-married couples lived and worked apart.

Supporting and motivating staff

Good working conditions alone won't motivate staff. When I ask individuals from the early days why ever they stayed, they'll give a number of reasons: the friendships they made, being part of the vision, the way they saw God moving, the excitement of being part of a team living on the edge and seeing things change, the environment of opportunity in which they could take risks and make mistakes while others helped them learn and grow.

Motivating factors

I ask myself, 'What motivates me?' and I use that to motivate others.

1. Activity My pet hate is being bored, so I made sure my staff's days were structured and full of things which stretched them. While they might have agreed that inactivity is demotivating, I suspect that by the time I'd finished, many of them longed for a little boredom from time to time!

2. Clear expectations from the beginning New staff will arrive with all kinds of questions from 'Where are the showers?' to 'Who's in charge and will I like them?'; from 'Is it safe to wander around this place at night?' to 'What's expected of me in a violent situation?' They need satisfactory answers to these questions quickly, so the kind of welcome and induction they receive may well colour their feelings about the project in the future. For one thing, if residents pick up that the new staff member hasn't a clue what she is supposed to be doing, all kinds of long-term trouble could result.

It's hard to stay motivated when you haven't a clue what is expected of you. Staff need a proper job description, given to them by the person who requires them to do the work. It's important to review these job descriptions on a regular basis and to address any communication problems or training needs which come to light.

Not only individual members of staff but the team as a whole need to know what is expected of them. Team meetings (see Chapter 12) help them work together towards a common purpose which all understand.

3. Vision Unless you believe in a project's direction and purpose, it's hard to keep giving it your time, energy, effort and money. Staff who have no idea where the project is going will become insecure, frustrated and demotivated. In order to keep their eyes above their own tiredness, above the conflicts and trials which wear them down, they need to hear from the person who has the vision, and I would say they need to hear daily. The vision needs to be communicated in a way which will lift them above the mundane, touch their hearts and show them why they would want to buy into it. Leaders might use Scripture, stories or testimonies, and also encourage others to share news of how the vision is working out.

It's no good simply restating the big vision over and over again. People need a realistic step-by-step strategy for how they will get there. If I kept proclaiming that we were starting five houses for prostitutes, but we had only two contacts, those working with me might well lose heart. I'd need to be saying something like, 'In three months' time we're aiming for six good contacts and then we'll start an outreach meeting with their friends. Around the same time I'll invite one to live in my flat. By next year we'll aim to rent a small refuge …' and so on.

If you are hoping to lead a project, this might be a good time to restate your vision in one sentence, then write down three practical steps you might use to assure your most sceptical staff member that this vision is attainable.

4. Balancing challenge and support Individuals are motivated to come and work for you by your vision and by a sense of challenge. Without any challenge in their lives, people feel frustrated and nothing much will happen. However, as business has found out, high challenge, if maintained over a long period, will always need high support – and in any work with the poor, challenge levels are likely to be high. If your staff are not to hate the work they first loved, if they are not to hate the people to whom they were called, they will need appropriate support.

The level of that support will vary from individual to individual. Alison, a mature Christian, did not require a huge amount of support long-term, but lacked confidence as she started to work with us – she needed a boost. Fred had years of experience of ministry with the poor but his previous work had turned pear-shaped, so he too needed extra support for a while. Michelle, though very gifted in pastoral care, needed high levels of support in some other areas, for example if she became involved in a violent incident or was put in charge of administering something.

These days each house has a leader whose main role is to support their staff. Residents know they should go to their key worker and not to this person with their problems. Staff support includes noticing when a staff member is unhappy, making time to talk and pray things through with them and taking appropriate action. Leaders are proactive in debriefing staff who witness a violent incident or who are disappointed after a resident runs off. We also run regular pastoral interviews for all our staff, which offer both support and training – more of them in Chapter 12.

When things went wrong at the Night Shelter and we took drastic action to put everything right again, I spent many hours with each of the staff on a one-to-one basis, supporting them and caring for them. After all, we were undertaking an enormously tough task! Staff will feel supported if they know that leaders are there for them, even if they fail. That doesn't mean being soft – they need to know they will hear the truth. My staff would say I was unremittingly tough in ensuring that they did whatever was needed to come through their problem, but they knew also that I would be there supporting them every step of the way.

5. Freedom to fail If your staff fear failure it will sap their motivation because they won't be free to experiment creatively. If the leaders encourage initiative, people will make mistakes and things will go wrong, but we learn from our mistakes. If leaders keep giving people opportunities, even when they fail – if they back the staff and help them through difficulties – then everyone involved will grow. Pretending that things are fine when they aren't will help no one. Staff need to know that it's OK to fall apart, that we will still love and support and value them.

6. Enjoyment It's important that the team should socialise together, enjoying team outings and team-building sessions, as well as sharing humour.

If staff are trained, motivated and supported, they will grow!

12
Training

When I started the project I assumed that everyone would start with the same knowledge and motivation as myself. Being young, I thought of everyone as my peers (or above). In fact I'd gained a number of skills, quite unconsciously. I'd imbibed my parents' good understanding of people and spent some of my childhood living in France where a large, rough school taught me further people skills.

I'd learnt a good deal about the Christian way to handle things from my first church and more while working in Hong Kong. So when one of my staff flatly refused to forgive a resident it shocked me, as it did if they expressed their emotions in ungodly ways or decided all of a sudden that enough was enough and flounced off.

Because I'd had to cope without any training in Hong Kong, I thought everyone could work out from the Bible exactly how to counsel a drug addict or someone who had been sexually abused, but it seemed they couldn't.

When God spoke to me so clearly, out on the golf course, about setting up four houses, he also said, 'Break down everything that comes naturally to you and give it away.' He was talking about training. I began to realise that what appeared to come naturally to me did not necessarily come naturally to everyone. I set about identifying those areas and designing a training course through which I could teach them, and ever since then training has become a passion for me. I love not only delivering my planned material but also answering questions as they arise and having a forum in which we can debate ideas.

I came to realise that people came on staff because they liked the way in which we worked and they wanted to learn from us. That's part of what leadership is about – identifying what makes you unique and communicating it to others.

We find there's nothing so exciting as corporate training in a team setting. You can take training so much further when you begin with a team who know and trust one another, who share loyalty, commitment and understanding. People not only see the point of what they are learning together, but soon they have opportunities to apply it on a practical level, supporting one another as they do so.

At first I took the whole team out of the working environment for a day's training every fortnight. As well as having enormous fun together, this built great strength into the project and proved life-changing for most of the individuals concerned. For one thing, they felt valued – no one else in the church enjoyed this level of teaching.

I thought hard about what I wanted to teach them. We looked at our own relationships with God because, when I stopped to analyse how I learnt to help people with serious problems, I realised I drew on my understanding of the way God deals with me, step by step. We looked at Scripture to find God's heart for the poor and his teaching on forgiveness, prayer and discipleship. We looked at all kinds of practical issues, and if I lacked expertise in any area I'd call on someone else to train us all. In the early days we were pretty clueless in certain areas. We'd take anorexics hill-walking, and would they walk up and down hills, by day and night, hoping to lose yet more weight!

We looked at basic symptoms and what might cause them. Sometimes we found members of staff exhibiting milder forms of eating disorders, controlling patterns of behaviour or even abuse in their own lives. We were able to deal with these things before they limited the staff's effectiveness too much. I invested hundreds of hours with some individuals, which I count as time well spent.

Staff meetings provided regular opportunities to talk through how everyone was feeling, to deal with any issues and problems, to overhaul procedures, talk about new ventures together and to give further training – spontaneous or planned. When the staff met together to pray, each would receive spiritual support.

Today people come from all over the country – and the world – to work and train on the project. A Polish girl who wanted to start a hostel for female alcoholics in her home town came to us first for on-the-job training, as did an English girl who has now gone to start a work among prostitutes in Copenhagen. Since David and I spoke in various churches in the States and other staff members visited Texas, many have joined us from the USA. In fact, team meetings have developed a decidedly American twang! I asked one couple from Texas who are here at the moment why they chose to come to England for training.

'We couldn't find any other training so intense,' Drew explained. 'The fortnightly team training covers counselling, evangelism, prayer and personal discipleship – all from a biblical standpoint – and yet it's more about Christian living than theology. It may start as head knowledge but straight away we're plunged into modelling what we've learnt for the residents. We're counselling, discipling and praying for them, helping them work through serious problems like addictions or eating disorders. We're out evangelising on the streets and at the Night Shelter. School's all very well, but living it takes you a lot deeper. God's calling me to church plant and the training here is so relevant.

'We're dealing with big issues all the time,' he continued, 'and sometimes they bring to the surface emotional wounds in our own lives. Communal living does that too – at times we'll react badly, or become irritable, or feel rejected. It's not comfortable, but then pruning isn't meant to be. It has a purpose, though. In the end you come out as a different person – far more fruitful. The good thing is that people here care about our walk with God, about how we're handling things at home and in our marriage. We receive personal discipleship through pastoral interviews, through living so closely with the team and through church house groups. And I've noticed how it strengthens the church to have so many of its members discipled in this way.'

In fact the project's training philosophy is to be found throughout the King's Arms. When we trained sixty small group leaders it had a radical effect on the whole church. Training has spilled even more widely through our going to speak in various settings – Stoneleigh Bible Week or an NFI leaders' conference, for example. We haven't done that much or always got things right – we've learnt most of what we know through the serious mistakes we made! But, despite the cost and mess and the smallness, something real is happening in Bedford. Ordinary young Christians are being trained for leadership. An ordinary church *is* caring for the poor – they do feel welcome. Sometimes the lives of individuals are freed and transformed and we see Isaiah 61 happening before our eyes. I long to impart something of this, to see it reproduced elsewhere.

Planning the training and support of staff

Because people of potential are likely to be motivated by the chance to enlarge their knowledge, skill, experience and character, one of the best and most constructive ways in which you can motivate your team is by developing them. You will need to ask the questions:

• What do I want my team to know?
• What is unique about the way I work, which I can pass on to them?
• What is more general? Can I ask (or train) others to train in those areas?

We use a variety of training methods, but seek to cover development in three main areas.

(a) People need to be trained for tasks and then do them under supervision. Training without doing will be forgotten and could lead to frustration. If someone learns how to counsel an abused person but does not implement that training straightaway, it's in danger of remaining as mere head knowledge. If, on the other hand, having trained someone, you set him to work without providing him with accountability or opportunities for feedback, then he may feel directionless or at sea.

(b) The person's character needs training.

(c) The person's relationship with God needs challenging and developing.

We use the following tools for training and support:

Pastoral interviews

I saw how Dave Devenish used these with the Frontier Teams and developed the idea further. Each person has an interview at regular intervals – whether these are a month or a week apart will depend on the staff member and also on the leader giving the interviews. One girl needed fifteen minutes every day for months, others a couple of hours every four weeks.

The first part of each interview is for listening to whatever the person wants to say, be that grumbles or uncertainties about his work, personal and counselling issues, relationship difficulties, spiritual problems – anything! This should be a safe place for them to fall apart if necessary! The leader can give honest feedback, review how the staff member is doing, help them set goals, bring support, encouragement, confrontation, prayer – whatever is needed. The pastoral interviews provide wonderful channels for honest communication on both sides and help to ensure accountability. They often bring problems to light, so that they can be addressed. They show up areas where further training or support may be needed. Perhaps most of all they help the staff member to feel valued, because a leader is taking time to help him or her to develop in all aspects of life.

Pastoral interviews were never an easy ride for staff. On one level they became the notorious subject of many jokes within the project, but most would do anything to have one, because they recognised this was a real, life-changing opportunity for growth.

Goal-setting

This could happen as part of a pastoral interview or else-where. People like to be part of a developing organisa-tion, especially when they themselves can contribute towards seeing its vision fulfilled. Again, you have to help them break things down into realistic, attainable goals, but first you will need to help them to assess where they are now. Having done that you can think together about where they would like to be in one year and then about how they are going to get there. To keep things concrete I ask them to choose three areas in which they can set themselves realistic targets. These have to be measurable, specific and attainable within a time limit. House leaders can then give them opportunities which will help them meet those goals.

I find the most satisfactory things about training are seeing the reproduction of ministry, seeing individuals enter into the fullness of all that God has called them to and seeing them equipped to fulfil the desires of their hearts.

13

Local Church and Ministry with the Poor

Who cares for the poor?

A Christian couple, Andy and Justine, invited an alcoholic to live with their family, but his repentance wavered and he slipped back to his old ways. As he still lived in their house, Andy and Justine bore the stress and responsibility without a break. They found themselves unable to set proper boundaries or to bring discipline to bear and could only watch their family and property being damaged as the situation deteriorated. They had acted unselfishly and in good faith but they became disillusioned, feeling that God had let them down and that their church wasn't much help either. They said they would never get involved with needy people again.

I wouldn't like to tell you how many times I've heard stories of Christians with compassionate hearts who try to take on needy people by themselves – and more often than not it ends in tears! I know from personal experience how tough it can be to take a seriously needy person into your home, where you are responsible twenty-four hours a day, for however long it takes. You invest so much that it's hard to remain objective and to let go when the people abuse you – and themselves.

To be honest, the probability of long-term change in any one highly damaged individual is not that high. If you can draw on a big pool of, say, sixty people, you're likely to see at least one (though probably many more) who becomes a true disciple of Jesus.

David and I believe very strongly that caring for the poor has to be the responsibility of the local expression of the body of Christ. A strong dynamic comes into play when a local church works with the poor, because God longs for the disadvantaged to become radical disciples of Jesus. That involves being built into his body – being knitted together with those who love him. He longs for churches full of people who were once broken, whom he has redeemed and restored and who go on to bring his restoration to others.

Other Christians care for disadvantaged people through para-church organisations. Sometimes these develop highly specialist care, e.g. people working with spina bifida. But though these organisations do an amazing job, even those with a Christian base are not normally linked to local churches. Para-church organisations may be able to offer effective physical care, but they will struggle when it comes to discipleship and to bringing the promises of Isaiah 61 into people's lives.

We remain clear that the Clarendon Street Project is fundamentally part of the King's Arms. It follows the vision and heart of that local church's leadership. David and I have moved to Birmingham now, but we have no doubts about the future health of the ministry we left behind. It's really important to choose carefully the church where you establish your vision!

Ministry with the poor is only one part of church life, but we believe it is a non-negotiable part. When we were looking at planting a church we asked ourselves, 'If Jesus were to start one here in the centre of Bedford, what would it look like?' We asked our house group as well. It wasn't long before someone said, 'It would reach out to include people standing on the street corners – the ones who have nowhere to sleep at night, the addicts, the "unemployable", the rejected.'

After all, Jesus announced at the start of his ministry on earth that God had sent him to 'bring good news to the poor, to proclaim release to the captives and recovery of sight to the blind, to let the oppressed go free, to proclaim the year of the Lord's favour' (Luke 4:18–19). Those words sum up the good news he brought. And where did he spend his time? With the prostitutes and sinners and lepers and blind people – with social outcasts and anyone pushed outside polite secular or religious society. When asked why he spent his time with outcasts, he replied that it's the sick who need a doctor.

Scripture says that God brings blessing to those who reach out to the poor. 'If you spend yourselves on behalf of the hungry and satisfy the needs of the oppressed, then your light will rise in the darkness, and your night will become like the noonday. The Lord will guide you always; he will satisfy your needs in a sun-scorched land and will strengthen your frame. You will be like a well-watered garden, like a spring whose waters never fail. Your people will rebuild the ancient ruins and will raise up the age-old foundations; you will be called Repairer of

Broken Walls, Restorer of Streets with Dwellings' (Isaiah 58:10–12).

A church where the poor are welcome

Jesus commanded in Luke 14:13, 'When you give a banquet, invite the poor, the crippled, the lame, the blind!' So, work with the poor is not an option, yet look at most churches in Britain today. They're not overflowing with marginalised individuals. In fact, imagine what would happen if a homeless person turned up at a church you know. Would that person feel comfortable?

When I first met him, David said he wanted to plant a church in which the poor were welcome. He'd thought the whole thing through in the years that followed. Knowing their concentration spans might not be as good as those of middle-class students and that they might not be used to sitting or standing in one place for very long, he programmed a break for coffee and doughnuts into the middle of our services, and made sure that sermons were kept short and rooted in real life.

There are implications and costs involved in inviting the poor to join the church to feast on God's word together, or enjoy worship and fellowship. James 2:2–5 says, 'Suppose a man comes into your meeting wearing a gold ring and fine clothes, and a poor man in shabby clothes also comes in. If you show special attention to the man wearing fine clothes and say, "Here's a good seat for you," but say to the poor man, "You stand there" or "Sit on the floor by my feet," have you not discriminated among yourselves and become judges with evil thoughts? Listen, my dear brothers: Has not God chosen those who are poor in the eyes of the world to be rich in faith and to inherit the kingdom he promised those who love him?'

The poor will bring blessing, but in the meanwhile how will the congregation and leaders react to any smells, noise or throwings-up in the middle of the service? If a homeless person became a Christian, who in the church would have the skills or time to help her untangle a shockingly messy lifestyle and discover her own value in Christ?

'How are you then, Steve?' I heard David ask in our church the other Sunday morning.

'Not so good. I'm gonna get sent down next week for sure.' Steve explained he'd been arrested for being 'drunk and disorderly' and that his case was coming before the magistrate the following Wednesday.

It's not unusual for someone to come along to the King's Arms, Sunday by Sunday, then to disappear to prison for a few weeks or months. 'That's the kind of church I want,' David explains to anyone who looks startled. 'We want these people to feel welcome. Many of them have met with Jesus, but that doesn't necessarily mean that their lives become ordered overnight. They'll be OK for a while and then they'll go on a binge of drinking or gambling or whatever. But most will return after their spell "inside" and perhaps they'll move on a bit further. Maybe it'll take years.' Steve's hung around the King's Arms for seven years, and he'll be back, because he knows our love for him is unconditional.

Around the time David planted the King's Arms, we were moved by a true story told by American sociologist Tony Campolo. In a twenty-four-hour café late one night he overheard a group of prostitutes talking and found out one of them had a birthday the next day. When she had gone he asked around a bit, organised a few things and the next night, at the same time, she arrived to find a surprise birthday party. She cried then, because someone had considered her as a person for once, but once she'd got over her tears, everyone thoroughly enjoyed themselves. Eventually they asked Tony what he did, and learnt he was a Christian. 'Funny Christian,' they said. 'What kind of church do you go to?'

Tony thought for a moment, then replied, 'The kind of church which would throw a party for a hooker at four in the morning.'

Placing ministry with the poor within the life of the church

Our church didn't start because a bunch of keen youngsters felt called to work with disadvantaged people – we can think of only three from the early days who joined us for that reason. No, David planted a church and taught us what the Bible said about the poor and marginalised. Neither he nor I tried to convince people that they should work with the poor, but we did look for people with a pioneering spirit and a willingness to come out of their comfort zones in order to embrace the life-changing works of Jesus.

We recognised that even the best-hearted people need time and space to think and pray before they take the plunge and dare to do! I too had needed a time of adjustment and counting the cost; a time to develop a deeper intimacy with Jesus. It's vital that all we do flows from his love.

I don't want to give the impression that the King's Arms is all about work with the poor. A church needs a strong base before starting a substantial ministry to the poor, otherwise that ministry will take over as the church's sole purpose in a way which wouldn't be right.

Three priorities on which David built the King's Arms were worshipping God (both in meetings and in life), building community and reaching the lost. We describe the church as a house, with a huge front door welcoming everyone inside and a big back door through which, having been trained and discipled, people can go out again to start other churches and ministries. And our favourite room in the house is the lounge, where people can relate together informally, like family.

Our house groups are central to church life, because we believe discipleship, pastoral care and friendship are so important. Our outreach includes Alpha-like groups and work in Bedford's colleges. We're also a sending church – we send out teams and individuals to support, train, teach, preach, prophesy or in different ways to resource other churches, both in this country and overseas. The King's Arms will contribute towards NFI's big church-planting initiative in the Midlands. In fact the King's Arms emphasises ministry with the poor far less than training people to church-plant and has already sent people, including its leaders, to do this in a number of places.

Leadership

A local church would be unwise to start a ministry (to the poor or any other) unless a gifted leader, with a vision, comes forward to run it. The role of the church is to equip the saints for every good work and to seek God as to where that church's sphere of service lies. Leaders won't do the work themselves but will facilitate others' visions when they fall within the parameters they have set. The project leader has to remain accountable to the church leaders, yet be mature enough not to go running to them every time a small problem occurs.

If church leaders become bogged down with the problems of broken people, they won't be free to take the church forward. Unless a project has several leaders of exceptional quality, we reckon that a church needs at least a hundred members to be able to sustain residential work with the poor. It will also need to be strong to withstand some of the problems which broken people will inevitably bring to light. If its leaders lack spiritual authority they will struggle to set the demonised free. If someone starts attacking members of the congregation or being divisive, then church leaders will have to deal with the situation and act decisively.

Once they have set a framework and a project is up and running, church leaders' on-going role is to affirm the project's workers and leaders and to keep the church's vision for it alive. That's not hard. On a Sunday David will make little references which include everyone, like, 'If you're at school or college, *if you're a resident in one of the hostels* or out at work, if you're a mum at home with small children or *if you're living on the streets*, then ...' He also asks people involved in the project to share their stories, which build faith. They also stimulate church members to pray, or to stop feeling sorry for themselves and volunteer some help instead. Church leaders will also get the whole church praying for the project at some of our prayer meetings.

What if you have a heart for the poor and want to see a ministry established in your local church? Maybe God is asking you to establish a work in the local prison or to start a soup run. You talk to the church leadership and they say, 'Sure, go ahead, recruit some people. We're right behind you!' It's important to be certain that they understand their responsibilities and the consequences for the church. If your team starts bringing ex-prisoners to Sunday services, that has consequences for your children's work, for the security of the building (rented or owned), for finance, for people resources, for counselling and prayer teams – the list is endless. If the leaders have given merely a passive assent, when problems hit, as they will, it will set the church reeling. Everyone will blame both you and them, since there will be no clear guidelines as to who is responsible for what.

If the church leaders themselves are passionate to establish a ministry to the poor, if they see this work as an essential part of church long-term – great! But if your project is not in the heart of the leadership, you cannot expect it to be central to the vision of the church. Working with the poor may appear to carry an air of glamour at first, but only from a distance! Something established with great enthusiasm as 'flavour of the month' may die just as quickly. That falls so far short of God's message of constant care that it may well leave the vulnerable worse off than they were before, spiritually as well as materially.

If you have a heart for the poor and the leadership of your church don't understand that or won't listen, then there are a number of possibilities:

- Your vision may be for later and God may be in the process of changing hearts within your church. All you can do is pray and find some way in which you can care for the poor – maybe for the widow and orphan next door. Don't try to bludgeon or cajole the leadership. The church needs their objectivity. Without it every person with a vision will assume that everyone else in the church should be behind it – and chaos will ensue!
- Your vision might be for a different church. Not every ministry can (or should) be established in every church.

Consequences to the church of ministry with the poor

When you work with the poor the questions start, so a wise church will think them through beforehand, because ministering to the poor causes violent repercussions in any church, involving both amazing blessing and extreme cost. Many things need thinking and talking through beforehand and the leaders need to prepare and train the church. Take stewarding, for example. Suppose someone you met on the soup run decides he wants to come to church, then urinates in the middle of the service. As the dampness and smell spread, do the stewards know what to do? Or if someone who can't control his anger snatches the kettle used to make everyone a friendly cup of tea and starts chucking boiling water over the congregation – who will deal with that? If an ex-prisoner runs off with the collection, how will your treasurer react? If someone is known to smell, be drunk, to have fleas or AIDS, will anyone sit within a ten-metre radius? Are you prepared for members' cars or the building where your church meets to be vandalised? All of these things have happened in our church, and more. Leaders of the project shouldn't attempt to deal with them in the church setting. It's the leaders of the church who have to stand up and say, 'What happened last week we welcome. We want it in our church, because the blessings here are the result of our love for the poor.'

When I had our son Edward, one of the midwives turned out to be a Christian and afterwards decided to visit the King's Arms. When she turned up with a 'minder' because she had heard it was such a dangerous place, David and I debated whether she was paying us a compliment or not! Our church has certainly experienced violent incidents ranging from mild – the chucking of chocolate Easter eggs – to serious – Pete, from the project's staff, had to stand between one of our family's teenagers and a man who had backed him against a wall and was threatening to kill him. It wasn't only the poor from the streets who caused trouble. Outside the church one day a woman punched me repeatedly on the side of my head. She lived on a private estate in Bedford!

Another time I was phoning to try and arrange a deposit on a bedsit for a homeless guy who had turned up at church, but while I wasn't looking he stole someone's handbag and ran off.

Other incidents, though not violent or criminal, alarmed everyone, as when a regular attendee at the local psychiatric unit stood at the front and started to remove his clothes. In the early days especially, screams and kicks from those troubled by demons were not uncommon. Broken people occasionally start manifesting when a church at worship leads them into the holy presence of God. It took us a while to discover how to deal with their demons in peace, preserving the dignity of the individual.

It's one thing welcoming damaged people, but if these kinds of incidents run out of control the church and, more importantly, the gospel lose credibility. When assorted unsaved members of David's and my families came to church to see our three children being dedicated, they weren't too impressed when a guy from the project threatened to throw paint all over the building.

We had to act responsibly towards the places where we met, too, which wasn't easy when a group took to prowling around the entrance lobby of the school where we were meeting, looking for a way to break the alarm system guarding the school's silver cups. On the same night it was tampered with, cars outside were vandalised. Unfortunately we were on our last warning because of previous trouble we'd caused in the school building. We had to find a different place to meet in quite a hurry! Sometimes we longed for a church building of our own. Yet when we'd had one, at Woodside, I worried that our contacts would torch it some dark night!

Although we're called to welcome everyone, violence, intimidation and law-breaking are not acceptable because the church needs to be a safe place for children, for mature Christians *and* for Night Shelter residents who turn up for the central heating and the coffee and doughnuts. Through various mistakes we made, we learnt that if the church leadership sets clear guidelines and boundaries, if they teach and train and put certain things in place, then the church will become safe and welcoming for all.

When David asked the most senior people in the church to form a security team, he explained that he felt they had the necessary clout to deal with situations and to call the police if need be – and they do, without hesitation. Also, just as we bar people from the Night Shelter for behaviour which repeatedly threatens the safety of others, so we bar people from church for the same reasons. That sounds harsh, but if the leadership of the church, as distinct from the leadership of the project, is not prepared to take decisive action, then everyone will get nervous about coming to church, especially if they feel their children are in danger. Given strong leadership, the church will grow. If leaders evade issues or put their heads in the sand, either the project will become detached or the church will suffer.

Leaders can prepare their church by:

- Teaching a biblical framework about God's heart for the poor.
- Laying out a clear vision of what is expected in their local situation.
- Training the church to receive the poor – helping them look at the biblical framework, then at the procedures and personnel needed. Once systems are in place, there is less room for violent or difficult situations to start.

Different parts of the church will need specific training, for example:

- Children's workers. (It's important to establish firm safeguards as to who works with children.) They may need training as they adapt the children's work to cater for the unsaved children of 'the poor' who come along.
- The stewarding team.

- The security team (which may need setting up to operate both outside and inside the building). They may need help establishing guidelines as to when to call the police etc.
- The prayer team. They may meet an increasing level of demonic activity and need to know how and where to handle it.

Accountability

The leaders of the project must of course be accountable to the church leadership – that's one of the great strengths of embedding work with the poor in the local church. Not only are there extra checks and balances for the work itself but for the staff, leaders and new Christians too, because a good church will know about all aspects of their lives. If someone's family is suffering because of his work on the project, for example, a good church will bring adjustment.

Before starting, though, it is really important to work out clear job descriptions and exactly who is responsible for what on a day-to-day basis. For example, is recruiting staff for the project the responsibility of the church or of the project leaders? Which decides who to accept as residents in the project? These things need talking through to avoid huge misunderstandings later. When David led the church and I led the project, it worked well because we were of one heart and mind. But who would ensure objectivity in a husband and wife team? So we appointed a council of reference from within the church leadership to oversee the project and ensure objectivity.

Who is responsible for the legal side and the finances? Day-to-day matters may well be down to the project leaders, but clearly they need to be accountable to the church leaders and trustees. We don't run a separate trust for the project, since we feel that would lead ultimately to its divorce from the church.

David always joked that the church trustees gave me enough rope to hang myself but not enough to hang them. It was my job to ensure that all the finances came in. The trustees and leaders of the church would have pulled the plug on the ministry if they decided it had become non-viable in terms of finance or the law. The health of the whole body of the church must come before the 'hand' or 'foot' of one branch of its ministry. Lopping off a part would be hard and painful, but not fatal.

Issues needing agreement

Male or female leadership? Married or single?

Caring professions tend to attract mainly female staff, many of whom go on to become skilled team leaders. Where churches develop caring ministries, this can become an issue. Some churches struggle to accept females in leadership of any kind, or feel that leaders should be in a stable marriage, rather than single. Others may be quite happy intellectually at the thought of young, single women running the project, then when it actually happens, find they are struggling emotionally. Our staff used to be predominantly female, but most residents in the Night Shelter were men. It was important to establish what the church leadership felt about a young single female counselling or imposing agreed rules on an older man. Was that right or wrong in principle? If wrong, who else was going to do it? If OK, what safeguards needed putting in place?

Counselling models

It is important that project and church leaders are in agreement as to how they perceive biblical counselling. The issues that arise when counselling the poor tend to be somewhat 'larger than life' when compared with normal church issues. Halfway through counselling a victim of traumatic abuse is not the time to start debating the legitimacy of counselling!

Overall aim and vision

It's really important that churches and project leaders all understand the vision and the thinking that lies behind it. You need to be asking questions like: What is your philosophy of ministry? What is the thinking that undergirds and directs your practice? What are you seeking to achieve? Is it physical care, evangelism or both? Or is it more educational? Do project and church leadership mean the same things by their stated aims? For example, if you open a soup kitchen, some may think you are expressing the gospel simply by giving food. Others may think the food merely gives an excuse to 'evangelise'. It's the project leaders who will have the detailed vision, but the church leaders need to be in agreement with their overall aim and the two groups to be in constant dialogue about how this is being implemented and communicated.

How the local church gains from having a ministry to the poor

I've written about the problems thrown up by welcoming disadvantaged people into a local church, and I don't want to minimise these, but we've found that the church gains tremendously from the project and vice versa. A large proportion of our church members have, at one time or another, been involved in the project – as staff, as volunteers or as residents. This means that their faith has grown as they've prayed in the money needed for specific things and seen God provide in miraculous ways at the very last minute. They've prayed for individuals and, against all the odds, have seen them change. They've been stretched and challenged in ways few people of their age have been and, with support, have come through much stronger than before. Now many of them would be able to tackle most things, lead most things even. As many of us move on to plant new churches elsewhere, it's not been hard to find new leaders for the church. They have already been tested in their lives as well as in their ministry. The project grows competent leaders and church-planters, fast!

Working on the project, people receive an intense period of practical, theoretical and biblical training. They have regular pastoral interviews and experience discipleship over all kinds of issues in their own lives. Living in community and/or working on the project throws up all kinds of attitudes, good and bad, which might otherwise have remained hidden. Both staff and residents receive support as they work these through, getting rid of the bad and developing the good.

It's tough, being on the project, but everyone is in it together. Teams are created and deep friendships made. This spills over into the church, where the norm for relationships goes deeper than that which might come from meeting only on Sundays and in mid-week house groups.

On the other hand, the Sunday meetings and house groups provide spiritual input and further opportunities to grow in worship, in discipleship and in understanding. When a resident prays for or encourages a staff member in the house group context, suddenly all the battles seem worthwhile. Residents from the project are included in a normal church life. They see families which work well and single people living pure yet fulfilled lives, free from addictions. Through the dynamic of shared worship they open up to joy and to pain, and the manifest presence of the Holy Spirit softens their hearts.

The church grows as those not involved 'hands on' with the project pray and intercede and hear God on our behalf. The church provides a reservoir from which the project draws. A number of church couples will take in a homeless person on nights when the Shelter has insufficient beds. Some people give practical help – making curtains, doing maintenance. Mature Christians from the church help with the pastoral interviews – these are usually former staff or residents who understand all the tricks! Residents particularly appreciate people from outside the project investing time in their lives.

Church members who learn to practise their spiritual gifts in the safe environment of a house group may have opportunities to use them when praying for people on the streets. The church grows as people reached by the project become Christians. This messy but exciting growth keeps us on our toes as a church. It keeps us dealing with real issues and ensures we stay utterly dependent on God, because often only he has the answers to the appalling problems in people's lives.

14

Changes and Developments

God has a habit of changing our plans! I'd never wanted to set up residential work with the poor but I found that God *will* put the lonely into families. Somehow he *will* have them cared for.

Problems won't be resolved through weekly home group meetings and church attendance. Like pre-school children, badly broken people need twenty-four-hour care. After all, it's in living with people that we learn what they do during their time off, how they dress, how they keep their room or kitchen, how they view sex, marriage, money, authority, work, family, relationships and the law. All these make great opportunities for discipleship and for modelling a godly lifestyle.

As the project grew, I encouraged staff members to develop their own vision. One started a prison ministry, another a work with single mothers. The trouble was, they were cushioned from the realities. They took staff from the project rather than recruiting and training their own. When things worked well at first, they thought their ministry was more successful than it actually was. When left to their own devices, many found they lacked the essential recruiting and motivating skills. If I'd not had children, then I could have stepped in and addressed the issues. As it was all I could do was to ensure that these people left the Clarendon Street project with enough staff to do its work. The spin-off projects folded one by one, though it's possible that the two I mentioned will start again on a better footing soon.

I've never seen our work with the poor as an end in itself, rather as a vessel to express God's heart. I hope it's a model – not *the* model, not a franchise or a clone-spawner – but *a* model which proves that an ordinary local church really can work with the poor. If something happens to bring about the end of our four houses, the King's Arms will still care for the poor, but that care may have to be expressed in a different way.

Once our church was made up mainly of singles in their late teens or early twenties. Caring for single men on the streets seemed only natural. Now that we have many young couples with small children, people are developing concerns for single mothers. Other churches will care for old lonely people, or address the race or refugee issue, or work with battered wives, or with deprived or disabled children. All of these and more are valid expressions of local work with the poor, but ultimately, genuine love and compassion will reach across any barrier of age or background. People will be drawn by the love of Christ.

Family

Another thing which appeared to change my plans was starting a family. People often ask how I combine work with the poor with looking after our children. As a married woman, I believed God called me to love him, love my husband and love the poor. As a married woman with children I believed he has called me to love him, love my husband, *love my children* and love the poor. That obviously had enormous ramifications for my work.

Looking back, I didn't always practise what I preach about godly priorities. In the early days I would make myself available to counsel residents at all hours, even though David and I needed to spend time together. I made us late for at least two much-needed holidays because I hadn't learnt to say 'No', or 'Later'! At other times I tried to shield David too much. He didn't know the half of what was going on in the early days. I found it a fine line to draw. For a project leader to run to him with every little problem would have been disastrous, but for me to venture alone into a violent situation in the middle of the night, I now realise was plain foolishness.

David and I are still learning about priorities. It's not easy when you believe in making your whole life access- ible. We chose Isaiah 58 and 61 as the readings at our wedding, because they sum up our common vision, our passion to see the kingdom of God extended among the poor, and we had no intention of letting them into only a little bit of our lives. We knew that total involvement was far more costly than clinical professionalism – we weren't after distant client relationships, we wanted family. Families mean financial commitment, they mean untidiness, inconvenience and disappointment at times, but God invented families and puts the lonely in them for good reasons.

What of our own family? When God gave us children

– three within twenty-two months – some women in the church felt I'd let them down because I stopped working full time on the project. 'You've set such an example of a radical woman in the church. Don't stop now – find childminders or something!'

They didn't understand why I'd cared for the poor in the first place. The only reason was out of obedience to God, and now he was calling me to look after my children. Once all three go to school full time he might let me do other things, but the motivation which drives me will always be obedience to Jesus. I've been bought with a price and am not my own any more!

I knew I had to lay down everything and serve my children with the same passion and zeal with which I'd served the poor. Meetings about the project had to fit around Edward's sleeps and I'd start work properly at 7pm, after he'd gone down for the night.

That I was able to stay involved with the project at all was for two reasons. First, the church paid me wages for the first time – enough so that I could pay someone to do my shopping, housework and laundry. Secondly, there was Anne. David and I were on a speaking tour in the States when we felt it was time to start a family. I told him, 'The only person I'd want to look after my children is Anne.' An extremely godly woman and real prayer warrior, she's had three children herself.

Meanwhile, back in England, God had spoken to Anne and she approached me on our return. 'I don't know where you are in this,' she said, 'but if you're going to have children I'd love to look after them for you sometimes, to free you up.' Anne took Edward four mornings a week and later helped me with the twins, too.

After having the children we became extremely vigilant when the Night Shelter ran out of room and sent us people, even though we knew they only sent those who were sober and with whom they had established a relationship of trust. We have to exercise wisdom as to what we do or don't expose our children to, but David and I feel that it is good for our children to learn about homeless people at first-hand, and to understand God's care and compassion for them. I don't want to be one to whom Jesus says, 'I was homeless and you didn't give me somewhere to sleep.' It was never once convenient, especially after having the children, but I do not feel that 'I was a stranger and you took me in' applies only to those without young children.

The next step

In 1996 David was asked to head up a church-planting initiative in the Midlands and we moved there at the end of 1998. People said, 'How can you leave the project, and the church you started, and go and live in the middle of Birmingham?'

Well, it's true that I've never had a desire to live in a big city, but I know it will be the best thing for me. Time and time again obedience to God has seemed like the craziest thing, taking me away from everything that's comfortable, from everything that other people seem to work towards. But in my experience the craziest places have always turned out to be the happiest, and deep down I know that a safe, comfortable lifestyle would bore me stupid.

I long to see God's kingdom extended. We miss the

people in Bedford, though relationships you build like that never die and a few came with us to help church-plant. David and I know that both the King's Arms and the project are in a better place now than they have ever been and we handed over to people whom we ourselves trained.

For although around 3,000 have stayed in the project's houses since we started, the work has by no means finished. Some contacts from the early days still haven't been set free but they hang around the project and maybe one day will learn to accept love and healing. Others have found a measure of stability – one man holds down a job as a bus driver, but we'd love to see him really walking with God. Some who have found healing for their brokenness are reaching out to others in Bedford, across Britain and abroad. They have in their turn become 'repairers of the breach, restorers of streets to live in'.

As we prepared to move to Birmingham, the Discipleship House was becoming two. Thirty people couldn't really live together as family and multiplication is a healthy thing. They managed the moves into two different properties brilliantly. The residents drew up a list of all the equipment and furniture needed and then prayed it in. You should have seen their faces when brand new fridges and beds started arriving on the doorstep!

As David and I got ready to leave Bedford, I had been wondering whether or not my close contact with street people was coming to an end and whether my heart for the poor would be expressed in caring for needy children. Then I woke one morning after a vivid dream. In it I had been walking down one of the main streets in Birmingham and noticed lots of homeless people. I'd wanted to say, 'It's all right, you can come back with me!' but realised that I had nowhere to take them. I awoke so choked with frustration that I started berating David with the need to plant a church that cared for the poor. As this was happening in the bathroom at seven in the morning, a time at which I'm not normally coherent, he knew this was incredibly important to me!

'I would suffocate in a church where the poor don't have a key part to play!' I said, quoting Galatians 2 at him. 'Peter, James and John required one thing of Paul and Barnabas when they were church-planting – to remember the poor – and Paul says he was eager to do that!'

'It's OK!' David said. 'The poor will always be central to the churches we'll plant. Your task would be to oversee that side of things and to train people.'

Release from darkness

There hasn't been a mass spiritual revival movement among the poor in Britain since the days of Wesley and Whitefield. In the past few decades, while the Salvation Army has won huge respect for their work, most evangelicals have dismissed ministering to the poor as 'social action' dispensed by 'liberal Christians' who don't take the Bible seriously. Why should that be, when Scripture is so clear about God's heart for the poor, so specific about his commands to us in that area? I suppose it's easy to settle into a cosy middle-class Christian culture and to become so immersed in it that we ignore the needs of those around us – we simply don't see them.

Maybe this is the time to wake up. God has blessed us. We've prayed and sung about revival – 'This is the year of the favour of the Lord'. If we long to see him comfort those who mourn and to release those in darkness, do we expect him to do it with a thunderbolt from the sky, or is it more likely that he is telling us it's time to take on the challenge of getting our hands dirty? Yes, it will cost us in terms of our lifestyles. It will be anything but convenient, but we will grow in terms of love and compassion and faith and all the eternal qualities that really matter. We will experience life in all its fullness.

I suspect the other main reason why people don't work with the poor is that they don't feel strong enough, or good enough. The problems seem so overwhelming that only a person with superhuman strength could tackle them. But from Hong Kong to Bedford I've found that God takes ordinary, flawed human beings, who make no end of mistakes, and uses them to do extraordinary things. So if you feel ordinary – be encouraged. If you feel you've made mistakes, or that the people you've tried to help have let you down, that's what happens along the way. It's quite normal. If you press on, allowing God to teach and to use you, he will. Not only will the scales be shed from your eyes but you *will* see those imprisoned in dark places released, the broken-hearted restored, the captives freed and the poor receiving good news – *really* good news!

If you are interested in working on the project, please write to:

King's Arms Project, King's Arms Offices, 97b High Street, Bedford MK40 1NE, or e-mail them at k.a.project@pipemedia.co.uk

Appendix 1

SAMPLE GROUND RULES

These obviously vary depending on the nature of the project, so I have included three so that you are able to get a feel for the differing emphases:

1. Ground rules for the Night Shelter.
2. Ground rules for the Hostel.
3. Ground rules for the Discipleship House.

Appendix 1:1

Ground rules for the Night Shelter

1. You are welcome to arrive at any time after 7pm, and to leave by 9am the following morning. If you arrive before 8pm or after 10.15pm, or you have a meal, then you are committing yourself to staying the night.
2. Alcohol is not to be brought onto the property. This includes the grounds.
3. Any behaviour that could make one suspicious of dealing is unacceptable, e.g. handing over money, talking about drugs.
4. You may be asked to go straight to bed if you are drunk or high, and may be refused entry if you do not respond to staff advice.
5. Abusive or threatening behaviour is not acceptable, and any behaviour that causes annoyance to other

occupants or in our opinion endangers the progress of other residents on the project is unacceptable.

6. Smoking is not permitted in the bedrooms, bathrooms or kitchen. Smoking is allowed downstairs only, in the lounges and corridor.

7. Please respect the privacy of others.

8. No personal TVs on in bedrooms. Noise levels are to be kept down between 10.15pm and 7am, i.e. TVs, stereos, radios and loud noises. TV in the quiet lounge will be turned off at midnight.

9. Visitors need to leave at 10.15pm if not staying the night.

10. You will be asked to go to bed at midnight.

11. Please treat all property, furniture, fittings and equipment with due respect.

12. Please respect our neighbours at all times and keep noise levels down when coming in and out.

13. TV programmes showing scenes of sex, violence or occultic activity are not to be watched in the Night Shelter.

14. All illegal or immoral activity is unacceptable.

15. Women are not to go into men's bedrooms. Men are not to go into women's bedrooms.

16. Only one person in a bathroom at any one time.

17. You are not allowed in the garden.

Appendix 1:2

Ground rules for the Hostel

NB: THE HOSTEL IS OPEN 7.30am–12.30am.
THE DOORS ARE LOCKED AT 12.30am

1. Everyone in the house needs to attend all monthly house meetings and emergency meetings.
   Reason: These are for your benefit and information. This is an opportunity for you to communicate your views, needs and comments.
2. Everyone within the house will be given a key worker and is expected to meet with them weekly.
   Reason: This is in order to provide you with the best care and to ensure that you find living here helpful.
3. Everyone within the house needs to pay £15 a week as a contribution towards food and heating costs.
   Reason: We want to be able to offer you the amenities here.
4. Please abide by the advice of the staff.
   Reason: The advice is for your benefit and for the safe running of the house.
5. Please have respect for everyone living in the house and our neighbours at all times.
   Reason: The more you show respect to others, the more likely they are to respect you.
6. Violence and physically or verbally threatening behaviour will not be tolerated.
   Reason: This is an unacceptable way to deal with problems and it is unfair to ask others to put up with it.
7. No weapons or implements that could be used as weapons are to be brought onto the property.
   Reason: We want to keep this a safe house.
8. If anyone comes back to the house affected by drugs, solvents or alcohol, they need to either go straight to their room or stay out until the effects have worn off.

Reason: Again, we want to keep this a safe house.

9. No alcohol is to be brought onto the property or consumed on the property.

   Reason: Drunkenness or behaviour that causes a nuisance severely endangers the progress of other residents and restricts your ability to uphold the ground rules of the house.

10. No substance abuse (drug or solvent) will be tolerated on the property.

    Reason: This is a safe house. These affect behaviour and can cause a nuisance, severely endangering the progress of other residents and restricting your ability to uphold the ground rules of the house.

11. No violent, occultic or pornographic videos (inc. all 18s), TV programmes, books or music are to be watched, read or listened to in the house.

    Reason: This is a shared house and this material is offensive to some people.

12. Do not use the house for any illegal or immoral activity.

    Reason: This will draw police attention and staff cannot support you in illegal activity.

13. Racist and sexist behaviour will not be tolerated.

    Reason: Everyone is equal, regardless of sex or ethnic origin.

14. Smoking is allowed only in Room 1 or outside the house.

    Reason: Smoking can be a fire and health risk and not everyone enjoys it.

15. Two guests are allowed per resident between 10.30am and 10.30pm (except during house meetings) and are welcome in the communal areas,

although staff reserve the right to ask people to leave.

Reason: It is a shared house and we need to remember that others live here too. Residents are accountable for their guests and need to take responsibility for asking them to leave if their behaviour is out of order.

16. No one is to go into the room of someone of the opposite sex, although staff may be required to for work purposes.

    Reason: We do not want to put vulnerable people at risk.

17. Noise should be kept at a reasonable level at all times. After 10.30pm the house is to be quiet (this includes TVs, stereo/radios and loud voices etc).

    Reason: This is the time when some people in the house, and neighbours, go to bed. Again, it is about respect.

18. Everyone who lives at the hostel goes on every rota, e.g. cooking, cleaning, washing-up etc.

    Reason: This is a shared house; we all need to share in the chores.

19. Each resident needs to do their share of cleaning. This includes their room, communal areas and keeping the kitchen tidy when you use it (see the cleaning rota).

    Reason: Again, we share the house and each person needs to play their part in keeping it clean.

20. Please keep to the set meal times and food guidelines on the kitchen noticeboard.

    Reason: We want to offer a reasonable menu which we can only do if food for meals isn't eaten at other times.

Appendix 1:3

Ground rules for the Discipleship House, May 1997

We want our home to be a place where there is love and security, where we know God intimately, and where we are committed to living lives of radical obedience to him. In order to create such an environment, certain rules and guidelines are necessary to ensure stability and safety.

1. Everyone within the house needs to attend house meetings, and fortnightly pastoral talks with appropriate team members.
   Reason: These meetings are for your benefit and information. This is an opportunity for communication and discipleship.
2. The use of illegal drugs and solvents or any illegal or immoral activity is unacceptable either on or off the property. Neither alcohol nor drugs are to be brought onto the property or used on the property. If you are found to be intoxicated you will be asked not to remain in communal areas.
   Reason: Ungodly behaviour is unacceptable; drunkenness or behaviour that causes a nuisance severely endangers the progress of other residents and restricts your ability to uphold the ground rules of the house.
3. Any form of self-harming behaviour is unacceptable on or off the property.
   Reason: Our bodies are the temple of the Holy Spirit and this is an ungodly way to deal with pain.

4. The possession of weapons or threatening or abusive behaviour will not be tolerated.

   Reason: This is an ungodly and unacceptable way to deal with problems and it is unfair to ask others to put up with it.

5. Guests are welcome between 9.00am and 10.30pm, unless an exception is cleared previously with the team. Team members have the right to refuse entrance for the protection of other residents and the house. You will be responsible for your own guests, their behaviour and what they bring into the house.

   Note:

   (a) Before inviting any contacts from the Night Shelter, Hostel or past residents, please clear with a team member first.

   (b) Entertaining of guests must take place in communal areas only, unless cleared with the team otherwise.

6. Each resident of the Discipleship House is responsible for cleaning their own rooms, keeping communal areas tidy after use and doing jobs on the rota, e.g. cooking, Saturday cleaning, washing-up.

   Reason: We share the house benefits and each person needs to take responsibility to keep it clean.

7. Smoking is permitted, but only outside the house in the designated area, which is at the rear of the house. Smoking is not allowed between the hours of 11pm and 7am for security reasons. In addition, smokers are asked to do smokers' duties as allocated on the rota.

   Reason: Smoking is a fire and health risk and not everybody enjoys it.

8. Please have respect for the privacy and needs of

everybody living in the house, and our neighbours, at all times.

Reason: To show consideration to others.

9. Noise levels should be kept at a reasonable level at all times and the house is to be quiet between 11pm and 9am (this includes TVs, stereos, radios and loud voices etc).

Reason: People in the house need to sleep and it is part of respecting one another.

10. Violent, occultic and pornographic videos, TV programmes, books or music are not to be watched, read or listened to in the house.

Reason: It is understood that if you want to live in this house you are wanting to pursue a relationship with God; therefore the above are ungodly, unhelpful and do not provide a safe environment.

11. No secular music is to be played in communal areas.

Reason: We want to create an environment in which we can all grow, and certain music is unhelpful to some people's needs.

12. Residents of the Discipleship House are to pay their rent in advance at the appointed time.

Reason: You are paying for a service; once you are in arrears it is hard to get up to date.

13. Residents are to be in the house and in their own rooms by 11pm for roll call.

Reason: Part of discipleship is personal discipline; we need to keep noise levels down to ensure that those who wish to sleep at 11pm are able to do so. .

14. Residents are asked to store all medication, both prescription and over-the-counter, in the medicine cabinet in the office.

Reason: Loose medication can be a temptation to other residents and is therefore a safety risk.

15. Residents are asked to co-operate with the team. Persistent failure to do this in some circumstances may mean you will be asked to leave.

Reason: The aim of the house is to grow into maturity as Christians. Therefore, when your behaviour consistently goes against this, we would understand you do not want to be discipled by us.

Signed by _____   Date _____

Witnessed by _____

Appendix 2

SAMPLE RESIDENT'S AGREEMENT

Discipleship House Resident's Agreement

Dear _____

Welcome to Discipleship House! Discipleship House is for Christians who are committed to growing in their walk with God and in righteousness. It is a place where residents are challenged to live daily by biblical principles. This agreement explains the basis on which we have granted permission for you to stay here. The accommodation is offered to you from _____.

1. You will be provided with the share of a furnished room, and have the use of the communal parts of the building which you are expected to keep clean and tidy.

2. The team have a right to entry to the room at all times. The team reserve the right to search personal property if they suspect possession of illegal substances, alcohol, theft or other items not allowed on Discipleship House grounds as covered in the Ground Rules. Should the team need to enter or search, this will be done in such a way as to respect your privacy as reasonably as possible.

3. The charge for the facilities provided is £80 per week and this amount includes the reasonable use of gas and electricity for heating, cooking, lighting etc., as

well as regular meals. It will be necessary to adjust this weekly payment if the gas and electricity is considered by us to be excessive. We reserve the right to alter rent charges at any time. If rent is to be altered, a notice period of two weeks will be given.

4. Payments must be prompt and regular every _____. We must be informed immediately if for any reason you are unable to pay part or all of the charges at the times stated. If you are waiting for housing benefit to come through as a means of paying your rent, then you will be asked to contribute your income support (or equivalent) towards your rent. Rent must be paid at least one week in advance, depending upon when you receive your funds.

5. The accommodation is offered subject to the condition that you agree:

   (a) Not to interfere with the personal property of any other person staying at the house.

   (b) Not to damage, remove, interfere with, alter or redecorate any part of the structure or the contents of the house.

   (c) Not to alter the inventory totals, or move any furniture from one room to another without prior consent.

   (d) Not to carry on any trade or professional business in Discipleship House.

   (e) Not to do anything whereby the Discipleship House insurance policy may be affected in any way.

   (f) Not to participate in any racist and/or sexist behaviour.

   (g) To abide by the house rules and biblical principles of behaviour.

(h) To keep your room open at all times. Keys must remain in the doors at all times.

6. There are certain circumstances in which you will be asked to leave.

(a) Failure to abide by the house rules.

(b) Continuing to occupy your room after the agreed date for leaving has passed.

(c) Failure to take reasonable care of your room and/or of the furniture, fittings and equipment in the room.

(d) Failure to comply with the conditions in paragraph 4.

If you are asked to leave, you will be given written confirmation and **under most circumstances** will have seven days in which to find other accommodation.

7. We are responsible for the repair and the maintenance of the room and the services, but you are responsible for any damage you cause. If you find anything that requires repair or replacement, you should report the matter to the team immediately.

8. We are not responsible for the loss of your personal property, neither is your personal property insured by us. When your occupation of your room ceases, you must arrange for the prompt collection of your personal property. If after ONE MONTH this has not been collected, we may dispose of it.

9. You are not to park or leave on any part of Discipleship House grounds any untaxed or uninsured vehicle, whether belonging to you or another, except for carrying out minor repairs. When your accommodation ceases you must remove all vehicles which you own.

10. We shall be under no obligation to find you alterna-
    tive accommodation when you leave.
11. If you have any complaints about any aspects of the
    project you should contact the Discipleship House
    team. If after this you still feel dissatisfied or feel
    that matters have not been dealt with sufficiently,
    you should contact [Name] in writing, who will
    ensure that your complaint is fully investigated.
12. All rights by this agreement are personal to you and
    give you no interest in land or right to exclusive use
    or possession of any part or parts of this property.
    This agreement does not create the relationship of
    landlord or tenant, or give you any rights such as a
    tenant would have.
13. During your stay at Discipleship House, detailed
    notes of your progress will be kept by the team.
    These notes, called PI Files, are the property of
    Discipleship House and will be retained by the
    House after the termination of your residency.*
14. A further clause may be inserted here dealing with
    any specific issue relevant to the individual resident.

I have read the agreement and agree to keep it.

Signed _____ (resident)

Signed _____ (on behalf of Discipleship
                          House)

Date _____

* Note to reader: refer to the Data Protection Act for guidelines
on keeping personal records.

Appendix 3

SAMPLE CONTRACT OF EMPLOYMENT

The King's Arms Project
97b High Street, Bedford MK40 1NE
Tel/Fax: (01234) 350664; E-mail:
k.a.project@pipemedia.co.uk

Contract of Employment

Dear
I have pleasure in offering you the position of Residential Volunteer Care Worker for The King's Arms Project. You will be resident at ....
Your duties and responsibilities will accord with the Job Description of the post, which is enclosed herewith.

Your employment as a Residential Volunteer Care Worker will commence on .... until ....

During the time you are employed you will be subject to the elders of The King's Arms church and the manager of The King's Arms Project.

You will need to be available to work on a shift system, with one day off per week and 35 additional days' holiday per year, to be agreed with the manager of The King's Arms Project.

You will not receive wages, and will contribute £.............
per week to cover rent. The King's Arms Project will

contribute £10 per week to cover food and bills excluding personal use of phone.

Termination of this agreement before the expiry of the term mentioned in paragraph 2 above may be made by mutual agreement, or in the event of serious breach of good conduct, following determination by the elders of The King's Arms church.

Yours sincerely

I have read the above agreement, and accept the position of Residential Volunteer Care Worker on the terms and conditions outlined above. I acknowledge receipt of the Job Description and a copy of this Agreement.

Signed .... Date ....

Appendix 4

SAMPLE HIV POLICY FORM

The King's Arms Project
97b High Street, Bedford MK40 1NE
Tel/Fax: (01234) 350664; E-mail:
k.a.project@pipemedia.co.uk

House Policy Regarding HIV III

1. All staff, residents and visitors will be regarded as having a positive AIDS test result.
2. The policy for anyone with an open wound is to cover it with a plaster, i.e. no open wounds.
3. If someone cuts themselves, they should cover the wound with a plaster, then clean up the spilt blood with bleach, wearing gloves.
4. Mop up any other body fluids, e.g. vomit, with bleach, wearing gloves.
5. Don't share razors or toothbrushes.

The King's Arms is a Christian church in association with New Frontiers International and a member of the Evangelical Alliance. Registered Charity No. 1044098

Appendix 5

SAMPLE MONTHLY ACCOUNTANCY SHEET

HOUSE NAME: MONTH:

	Monthly		Cumulative	
	Actual	Budget	Actual	Budget
Receipts:				
Rent and housing benefit				
Donations				
Grants				
Interest				
Payphone				
XS petty cash				
Miscellaneous				
*Previous year's receipts				
*Transfer from Building Society				
*Transfer from other houses				
Subtotal A:				
Expenditure:				
Petty cash				
Rent repayments				
Repairs/renovations				
Communal area repairs				
Property costs				
Water/electricity/gas				
Tithe				
Admin: Stationery				
Christmas				
Insurance/C. tax				
Phone				
Project Admin.				
Miscellaneous				
*Transfer to Building Society				
*Transfer to other houses				
Vehicles				
Subtotal B:				

Appendix 6

SOURCES OF FUNDING IN THE UK

1. Hostel status and benefits If you are seeking to run a discipleship house or a halfway house, you are not actually providing a form of recognised care. You are merely providing housing in a caring environment. Therefore those who live in your house are eligible for normal benefits, e.g. Housing Benefit, Unemployment Benefit etc.

The key things for you to do are to:

(a) Ensure that your house has hostel status (see the planning dept).

(b) Ensure you charge an adequate rent to cover the running costs of the house.

It is worth:

(a) Inviting your Housing Benefit Officer round to assess the property.

(b) Ringing other local hostels to see what they charge per week.

2. Housing Associations The standard way of financing hostels is through a Housing Association, e.g. Shaftesbury, Addullams, Pilgrims Housing etc. The Government allocates money through Housing Associations, and new projects then bid for it. Larger projects tend to be more successful but it is a hit or miss affair. However, successful candidates will be able to bid for:

• Capital funding costs.

• On-going funding where bed spaces are full.

3. Residential care homes This status is for those who wish to provide specialist nursing care, e.g. for the elderly or the mentally handicapped. The only way into this is via the social services. If you contact them explaining what it is you are wanting to do, they will have all the information you need.

Routes 2 and 3 are lengthy and you may find you are unable to sign some of the necessary equal opportunities documents. For those who have potential projects that match the criteria, they can be good routes to pursue.

4. European funding Certain areas of the UK have been identified as being in particular need of development and projects there may be eligible for funding from Europe (see your Council).

5. Grants, donations and gifts Your local library will have a large book containing a full list of all the Trusts which will fund particular types of project. It is worth asking a third party to handle this for you.

NB It is worth remembering that if your project comes under the charitable status of your church or if you set up your own charity, then you can take advantage of tax relief on donations, covenants, gift aid etc.

6. Social services funding When you are established and have a track record of working effectively, it is worth approaching the social services and enquiring about grants.

Further Reading

Altman, Roger, *Counselling in the Community* (Kingsway, 1996).

Altman, Roger, *Through the Counselling Maze* (Kingsway, 1996).

Cormack, David, *Seconds Away* (MARC/Monarch Publications, 1986).

Pullinger, Jackie, *Chasing the Dragon* (Hodder, 1980).

Pullinger, Jackie, *Crack in the Wall* (Hodder, 1989).